the HOME BAKER

the HOME BAKER

BAKER

THE GUIDE TO BAKING ALL THINGS SWEET AND SAVORY

Jacqueline Bellefontaine

This is a Parragon Publishing Book
First published in 2006

Parragon Publishing
Queen Street House
4 Queen Street
Bath BA1 1HE, UK

ISBN: 1-40548-036-X

Printed in Thailand

Created and produced by the Bridgewater Book Company Ltd

Picture acknowledgments
Jupiterimages Corporation page 32 (top) and 33.

NOTES FOR THE READER

This book uses imperial, metric, or US cup measurements. Follow the same
units of measurement throughout; do not mix imperial and metric. All spoon
measurements are level: teaspoons are assumed to be 5 ml, and tablespoons
are assumed to be 15 ml. Unless otherwise stated, milk is assumed to be low fat
and eggs are medium.

Nut allergies

Some recipes contain nuts. If you or your children are allergic to nuts you
should avoid contact with nuts and any products containing nuts.

CONTENTS

introduction

This book could not begin without an introduction to the basic principles of baking. On the following pages you will find all the information you need to bake cakes, pastry, and cookies with great success. You will be guided through the fundamentals of cake baking from greasing and lining the pan, to cake-making methods, and will be able to answer that all-important question, "Is it cooked?"

Discover the rules of great pastry, tips for fabulous-tasting cookies, and all there is to know about yeast. As if that were not enough to set you on the path to baking bliss, an indispensable "What went wrong?" guide will clear up any baking misdemeanors, so that you can be assured of perfect results each time you bake.

INTRODUCTION

Few other areas of home cooking are greeted with the same enthusiasm as baking, not just by home bakers themselves, but also by those who are lucky enough to be on the receiving end of home baking. Be they crisp, mouthwatering cookies, freshly baked bread rolls, or satisfying and comforting cakes, nothing quite beats the quality of home-baked goods. Everybody loves the flavor of cakes and buns still warm from the oven, and the aroma of freshly cooked breads is one of life's great delights.

However, many people are put off baking because they think it is difficult or too time-consuming. That is, happily, not the reality. Fabulous baked cakes can actually be mixed in just a few minutes, with only a modicum of skill needed, and can be lifted fresh from the oven in less than 30 minutes. A basic loaf of bread may take a little longer to produce, but often will not demand a great deal of active preparation time from the cook. Of course, some baking requires more time and skill, but the joy of *The Home Baker* is that there is something for everyone. Whether you want to produce a quick cake for tea or spend time creating an elaborate gateau that really challenges your baking skills, you will find the ideal recipe in this comprehensive baking book. Novices who need to be guided step by step through the recipes and more accomplished cooks alike will soon discover that the rewards of baking outweigh the effort involved, especially when it comes to other people's unfailing appreciation of the results of your labors. After all, baking is meant to be a sharing, uplifting experience!

While to become an outstanding home baker does require a certain amount of flair and inventiveness, baking is a science as well as an art, so unless you are very experienced, it is important to follow the recipes exactly. Read through the recipe and collect all the ingredients and equipment together before you start. Do not be tempted to cut corners. It is worth noting that there are some variables that may affect the end result, and this is where skill and experience come in. The biggest of these is usually the oven. Because oven temperatures can vary from appliance to appliance, to ensure the best results, use the baking times specified in the recipes as a guide only. Do not be tempted to check the oven too early, which could adversely affect the baked goods, but do check just a few minutes before the end of

the baking time to see how the baking is progressing. And if the food is not ready at the end of the baking time, bake for a little longer. If you are new to baking or not familiar with your oven, it is a good idea to bake a tray of cupcakes or a Victoria Sponge Cake as a test run. If these cook too quickly, your oven may be operating a little hotter than the controls indicate, so either lower the oven temperature slightly or check the baked goods a little earlier than the specified time. Likewise, if the cakes take longer than expected to bake, your oven may be a little slow, so increase the temperature by a few degrees.

Most importantly, remember that baking is a fun and highly rewarding pastime, so let that knowledge encourage and inspire you to go ahead right away and prepare your own home-baked creations today.

GETTING STARTED

EQUIPMENT

Measuring cups, mixing bowls, a wooden spoon, a few baking pans, and a rolling pin are all the items you need to begin baking. But as the baking bug bites, you can gradually add other tools to those basics, such as an electric whisk, which, although not essential, will certainly make the job easier and quicker.

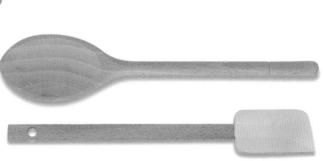

MEASURING

For successful baking, it is essential to have accurate measuring scales or cups and a set of measuring spoons. Electronic or balance scales are more accurate than measuring cups, which measure ingredients by volume. If you intend to do a lot of baking but generally use cups for measuring, it is worth investing in a set of scales to ensure success every time. It is important to bear in mind that spoon measures are always level unless otherwise stated in the recipe.

MIXING, BEATING, AND BLENDING

BOWLS

You will need a selection of bowls of various sizes. Choose from ceramic, glass, or stainless steel.

SPOONS

Wooden spoons come in a variety of sizes and are essential for beating ingredients together. A large metal spoon is useful for folding in flour.

SPATULAS

Plastic or silicone spatulas are ideal for scraping out bowls with the minimum of waste, as well as for folding in flour.

Tart pan

Cake pan

Springform cake pan

BAKEWARE

It is advisable to invest in a few good-quality baking pans. If looked after, they will last a lifetime, and they are less likely than inexpensive pans to twist or buckle in the oven and to cause sticking or burning. Choose ones that feel relatively heavy and do not bend easily.

The most useful to begin with are:
- Cookie sheets
- 7 inch/18 cm shallow cake pans
- 8 inch/20 cm shallow cake pans
- 9 inch/23 cm shallow cake pans
- 8 inch/20 cm deep loose-bottom or springform pan
- 8 inch/20 cm square cake pan
- 1 lb/450 g and 2 lb/900 g loaf pans
- 12-hole muffin and bun pans
- Jelly roll pan
- 8 inch/20 cm tart pan

WHISKS AND MIXERS

Electric appliances take the hard work out of creaming and whisking cake batters. A hand-held electric whisk is sufficient for cakes, while a free-standing mixer is useful for those who like to bake in larger quantities and for making bread. A manual balloon whisk is good for whisking egg whites and for whisked sponge mixes if you don't have or don't want to buy an electric whisk.

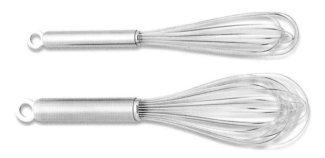

FOOD PROCESSORS

These are great for rubbing fat into flour quickly and efficiently. They can also be used to prepare cake batters, but tend not to incorporate as much air as mixing by hand or with a whisk, so the resulting cakes may be more dense.

INGREDIENTS

FLOUR

Wheat flour is the most commonly used flour for baking. The amount of gluten (protein) in wheat flour varies between the different types:

● **ALL-PURPOSE FLOUR** has the bran and wheat germ removed, and is then fortified with vitamins. Soft all-purpose flour is made from wheat with a low gluten content. It has a fine texture and is ideal for making cakes, pie dough, and cookies. White bread flour is milled from wheat with a high gluten content and is used for breads and most yeast cooking.

● **SELF-RISING FLOUR** is all-purpose white flour with baking powder added as a raising agent. To make self-rising flour add 2 teaspoons of baking powder to each scant 1⁵/₈ cups all-purpose flour.

● **WHOLE WHEAT FLOUR** is flour that has been milled from the whole of the wheat grain. It is coarser and heavier than white flour. It is available as a strong (high-gluten) flour for bread making and a soft (lower-gluten) flour for cakes and pastry.

● Other flours such as brown flour, malted flour, corn flour, and buckwheat, rye, rice, and chestnut flours are also sometimes used to a limited extent in baking, each having its own unique characteristic or flavor.

SUGARS

Most sugar is produced from one of two sources: sugar cane or sugar beet. There are a number of different types of sugar, each with its own particular qualities. Unrefined sugars are made from sugar cane and have a higher mineral, vitamin, and trace element content than refined sugars.

● **GRANULATED SUGAR** can be used to achieve a crunchy texture in some cookies and in cakes prepared by the rubbing-in method.

● **SUPERFINE SUGAR** has a finer crystal and dissolves more readily. It is the type of sugar most frequently used in baking. It is also known as caster sugar because it is suitable for placing in a caster–a container with a perforated top, similar to a flour sifter. Because it dissolves readily it is perfect for making meringues. It can be substituted for granulated sugar cup for cup.

● **GOLDEN GRANULATED SUGAR, GOLDEN SUPERFINE,** and **GOLDEN CONFECTIONERS' SUGAR** are unrefined forms of the refined sugars.

● **MOLASSES SUGAR** is a dark, fine-grained unrefined sugar from Mauritius that is used for rich fruit cakes. This unique sugar contains the highest amount of natural molasses of any sugar, resulting in an extra rich flavor and moistness. Molasses syrup is the dark-colored syrup that is left over after sugar has been refined. It is very concentrated, so only a small amount is required. Store molasses in tightly sealed containers at room temperature or in the refrigerator.

● **RAW BROWN SUGAR** is a large, coarse-grained brown sugar that can be made from either refined or unrefined sugar. As well as being used in baking, it is sometimes sprinkled over the tops of pies, crumbles, and cakes for its crunchy texture.

● **LIGHT** and **DARK BROWN SUGARS** are similar to light and dark muscovado sugars. They are usually refined white sugar that has been tossed in molasses or syrup.

● **CONFECTIONERS' SUGAR** has a fine, powdery grain and dissolves almost instantly. It is used in some cookies and pastry, and for making frostings and fillings.

FATS

● **BUTTER** produces the best flavor. Unsalted butter is generally considered best for baking. If you do use salted butter, you will not need to add any extra salt to the recipe (except for bread making). Use butter straight from the refrigerator for pastry making and at room temperature for cake making.

● **MARGARINE** is preferred over butter by some people for baking. Block margarine is generally the best to use, but soft margarine is needed when making cakes by the all-in-one method.

● **LOW-FAT SPREADS** are not suitable for baking, as they contain a high proportion of water.

● **SUET** is used for making suet crust pastry and can be made from either shredded beef fat or solidified vegetable oils.

● **SHORTENING** and **WHITE VEGETABLE FAT** have a bland flavor, but give a light, short texture to pastry and cookies, so are sometimes used. They are usually combined with butter for flavor.

EGGS

The size of eggs used in baking is important. Store eggs in the refrigerator away from strong-smelling foods. Remove from the refrigerator to return to room temperature before using if possible, as cold eggs do not combine as well with other ingredients or trap as much air.

RAISING AGENTS

● **BAKING POWDER** is a mixture of cream of tartar and baking soda. When mixed with moisture, it releases carbon dioxide, a harmless gas that expands during baking to make the food rise.

● **BAKING SODA** produces carbon dioxide when mixed with an acid such as lemon juice or buttermilk. It should always be mixed with other dry ingredients before the liquid is added.

● **YEAST** is a single-cell organism that converts the natural sugars in flour to produce carbon dioxide. Yeast needs warmth, moisture, and food (sugars) to work. It is available in both dried and fresh forms for baking.

CAKES

Homemade cakes bring immense pleasure to both the maker and the consumer. If you are new to baking, start by making some of the family cakes and cupcakes in this book. These are some of the most basic and easy-to-prepare cakes, which are nonetheless attractive and flavorsome, and are ideal for an everyday teatime treat, for packed lunches, or for a snack. Scones, breads, and muffins also fit this bill, and children especially will love to eat these. You could ask them to choose which small cakes to bake for themselves and the rest of the family. Once you have mastered the basics, you can move on to some of the more challenging cakes and gâteaux, perfect as a centerpiece for a special occasion or as a sumptuous dessert for a dinner party.

GREASING AND LINING CAKE PANS

Unless you have nonstick bakeware, you will need to grease your baking pans before using, and you may prefer to take the extra precaution of greasing nonstick pans in any case. What fat you use for greasing the pans is a matter of personal choice. A little butter or margarine can be smeared onto the pan, or use a light-flavored oil such as sunflower-seed, corn, or vegetable oil, brushed over the inside surface of the pan with a pastry brush. Whichever you use, the pan just needs to be very lightly coated.

Some recipes require the baking pan to be lined. In some cases, only the base of the pan needs to be lined, which helps to ensure that the cake is successfully turned out. Use waxed paper or nonstick parchment paper to line the pans.

It is essential to follow a cake recipe exactly and measure all ingredients accurately. Do not open the oven door too often, close the door gently, and move pans carefully.

Always preheat the oven before you begin preparing cakes. It is important that they go into the oven at the correct temperature and very few cakes will benefit from standing around for long while waiting for the oven to heat. Also grease any baking pans before you begin.

Most cakes will freeze well for up to four months without filling or frosting (although butter frosting freezes well). Most will keep in an airtight container for a few days, although some baked goods are best eaten on the day they are made.

LINING A CAKE PAN

ROUND PAN Place the pan on the paper and draw around it. Cut out the circle just inside the drawn line. Cut a strip of paper about $3/4$ inch/2 cm wider than the depth of the pan and long enough to go around the pan. Fold over about $1/2$ inch/1 cm along one long edge and snip from the edge up to the fold at $3/4$-inch/2-cm intervals along the length. Lightly grease the pan and position the strip of paper around the edge so that the snipped edge lies flat on the bottom of the pan. Lay the disk of paper in the bottom and lightly grease.

SQUARE PAN Proceed as for a round pan, folding the strip at the corners and snipping up to the fold so that the paper lies flush to the pan.

For rich fruit cakes, extra protection is needed to prevent the edges from burning or drying out during the extended cooking time. Line the pan as above, but use a double thickness of paper. Cut a double-thickness strip of brown paper about $3/4$ inch/2 cm deeper than the pan. Wrap around the outside of the pan and secure with string.

LINING A SHALLOW BAKING OR JELLY ROLL PAN

Cut the paper about 3 inches/7.5 cm longer and wider than the pan. Lightly grease the pan and place the paper on top. Snip at the corners and press into the pan. Lightly grease the paper.

LINING A LOAF PAN

Lightly grease the pan. Cut two strips of paper, one the width of the pan and long enough to cover the sides and bottom, and one the length of the pan and long enough to cover the bottom and sides. Press each piece into place and lightly grease.

CAKE-MAKING METHODS

The main ingredients for making cakes are flour, fat, sugar, and eggs. The proportion of fat to flour will influence the method by which the cake is made. With half or less fat to flour, the rubbing-in method is used, while with half or more fat to flour, the creaming method is used. If little or no fat is used, then whisking is the appropriate method.

CREAMED CAKES

The most well-known of cakes made by this method is the Sponge Cake, which uses butter, sugar, eggs, and flour in equal quantities to make a light and airy cake. It makes a good base for many variations. Cakes made by this method should have a light, even texture. The higher the proportion of fat, sugar, and eggs to flour, the richer the cake will be.

SPONGE CAKE

$3/4$ cup unsalted butter, softened

scant 1 cup superfine sugar

3 eggs, beaten

scant $1^1/4$ cups self-rising flour

BASIC METHOD

1 Cream (beat) the fat and sugar together in a bowl until pale and fluffy. A wooden spoon or a hand-held electric whisk is ideal for this task. The more thoroughly the fat and sugar are creamed together, the lighter the texture of the cake will be. Creaming also breaks down the sugar crystals, giving a finer texture. Use sugar with small crystals such as superfine or light brown sugar rather than the coarser granulated or raw brown sugar, as these will blend with the fat more easily.

2 Gradually add the eggs, beating well after each addition. Eggs are best used at room temperature. Add any flavoring extracts at this stage.

3 Sift the flour and any other fine dry ingredients. Carefully fold into the cake batter. Use a large metal

spoon or a spatula to do this and take care to incorporate the flour gently without knocking out the air you have beaten into the batter. Use a cutting and folding-over movement.

STORAGE Cakes made by the creaming method keep well in an airtight container. Undecorated cakes freeze well.

ALL-IN-ONE CAKES

This is a simplified variation of the creaming method. All the ingredients are beaten together at once until smooth. Extra baking powder helps to make the cake rise and soft margarine or butter is essential for it to mix fully. This gives a close-textured cake and is an ideal method when time is of the essence.

WHISKED SPONGE CAKES

Whisked sponges depend on the amount of air trapped into the eggs and sugar during the whisking of the eggs. The bowl should be warmed and the eggs at room temperature. The best results are achieved by using an electric whisk. Care then has to be taken not to knock the air out when folding in the flour, which must be done with a lightness of hand.

JELLY ROLL CAKE

3 large eggs
scant $2/3$ cup superfine sugar
scant 1 cup all-purpose flour
1 tbsp hot water

BASIC METHOD

1 Put the eggs and sugar in a warmed bowl and whisk together until very pale and thick. Air will become entangled with the albumen in the egg white and the mixture will increase considerably in volume. A good test to see if you have whisked in enough air is to try to write your initials with the mixture dropping from the whisk. If the mixture holds its shape long enough for you to write two

CURDLING IN CAKE BATTER

Curdling is the term used when the water from the eggs separates out from the fat globules in the cake batter,

and is usually caused by the eggs being too cold. A curdled cake batter will hold less air and will produce a cake with

a dense texture. To help prevent curdling, use eggs at room temperature. If your batter does begin to curdle, beat in a

tablespoon of the flour to help bind the mixture back together. This is not a true curdling, which is the process of

separating the curds from the whey in milk.

incorporates air. Liquid is added and the mixture is then gently brought together. Be careful not to overwork the batter or the results will be tough.

SCONE MIXTURE

scant 1⅝ cups self-rising flour
6 tbsp unsalted butter, cut into small pieces
1 tbsp superfine sugar
pinch of salt
1 egg, beaten
¼ cup milk

BASIC METHOD

1 Sift the flour into a bowl.

2 Rub in the fat with your fingertips, lifting your hands high to help to incorporate air into the mixture. The mixture should resemble fine bread crumbs.

initials before they disappear, the mixture is thick enough. Setting the bowl over a pan of hot water can help speed up the process.

2 If the mixture has been whisked over hot water, remove from the heat and continue whisking until it is cool.

3 Carefully fold in the sifted flour with a large metal spoon or spatula using a cutting and folding-over movement, blending with a little water.

4 Drizzle over any melted butter or oil specified in the recipe and carefully fold in.

STORAGE Fat-free sponges are best eaten on the day they are made. Those with some fat will keep a little longer if stored in an airtight container.

RUBBED-IN CAKES

This method of cake mixing produces a plain, coarse texture and is often used for breads, scones, and buns. The proportion of fat to flour varies from 25 percent to around 66 percent. Rubbing in the fat with the fingertips held high over the bowl

3 Stir in the sugar and any other dry ingredients used to flavor the scone, such as coconut or fruit.

4 Stir in the egg and milk.

STORAGE Rubbed-in cakes such as scones should be kept for no more than three days, as they tend to become dry over time.

MELTED CAKES

A few dense, moist cakes such as gingerbread employ this method. The fat and sugar are melted together before the dry ingredients are stirred in. Bake well in advance as this will improve their flavor. As a cookie, gingerbread can be made into a thin, crisp cookie (often called a gingersnap) or a thicker, softer cookie.

GINGERBREAD

1 lb/450 g all-purpose flour

1–2 tsp baking soda

2–4 tsp ground ginger

1 cup unsalted butter

scant 1 cup sugar (molasses
    or syrup)

BASIC METHOD

1 Sift the flour, raising agent, and ginger into a bowl.

2 Melt the fat, sugar, and/or syrup in a pan over low heat until the mixture combines. Take care not to overheat.

3 Pour into the dry ingredients along with any other liquids that are used.

4 Beat to form a smooth batter consistency.

STORAGE These cakes are best if left for one day before eating to become moist. They keep well in an airtight container.

SMALL CAKES

The same basic principles and techniques for making large cakes also apply to small cakes. However, the oven temperature is usually higher and the baking time much shorter. Small cakes, each not much more than a couple of bites in size, can be cooked in a 12-hole bun tray. For more substantial individual cakes, a muffin tray can be used. Lining the pans with paper cake cases will ensure that they turn out easily. Some small cakes are made as one large cake and then cut into appropriately sized bars or squares. This is a quick way of producing individual cakes. Small cakes should be simply decorated or left plain.

IS IT COOKED?

Follow the timings in the recipe as a guideline, but also rely on your own judgment, as ovens vary in temperature. Small cakes should be well risen, firm, and springy to the touch, and sponge cakes should also be springy to the touch.
Test by gently pressing the cake with a finger. Once you have removed your finger, the cake should spring back, but if you can still see the fingerprint, return the cake to the oven for a few minutes longer. Fruit cake and deep sponge cakes are best tested with a skewer, inserted into the center. The skewer will come out clean when the cake is cooked.
For most cakes, let cool for a few minutes in the pan before turning out and transferring to a cooling rack to cool completely. Some cakes such as rich fruit cakes benefit from being allowed to cool completely in the pan—the recipe will specify this where necessary.

PASTRY

Basic pie dough is not as difficult to make as is sometimes perceived, and although preparing other, more specialist pastries is an area of baking that does require a certain amount of skill, by following the recipes closely, that skill can be acquired and professional results achieved with a little practice.

It is important to follow a few basic rules when making pie dough. Always measure the ingredients accurately and keep everything cool. Always use a light touch and handle the dough with care. Knead the dough just sufficiently to bind it together—over-kneading will start to develop the gluten in the flour and result in a tough, greasy pastry.

Roll out pie dough lightly, taking care not to stretch it unduly. Use only a small amount of flour when rolling out to avoid upsetting the careful balance of ingredients. Allow the dough to rest wrapped in the refrigerator before rolling.

A little salt may be added to bring out the flavor of pastry, but if salted butter or margarine is used, this is usually sufficient.

COOKING PIE DOUGH

The oven must be hot when the pie dough is first put in so that it will rise when the air that it contains is heated. The gluten in the flour absorbs the water and stretches and entangles the air in the dough as the air expands. The heat of the oven then sets the pastry in its risen shape. As it cooks, the starch grains in the flour will also burst and absorb the fat. If the oven is too cool, the fat will melt and run out while the flour remains uncooked, resulting in a heavy, soggy and greasy pastry. After the pastry is set, the temperature can be reduced to cook the filling, if required.

TYPES OF PASTRY

All kinds of pastry, except suet crust, use all-purpose flour. Whole wheat flour can be used instead of white, but it produces heavier results and requires extra liquid to bring it together.

SHORT-CRUST PASTRY

Perhaps the most common home-baked pastry, this is also one of the easiest to master as long as the basic rules of pastry making are followed. A proportion of half fat to flour is used.

8 tbsp unsalted butter
scant 1⅝ cups all-purpose flour
2-3 tbsp cold water

BASIC METHOD

1 Sift the flour into a bowl.

2 Cut the fat into small cubes and add to the flour. Rub in using your fingertips, lifting your hand high above the bowl to incorporate more air. The mixture will resemble fine bread crumbs when the fat has been fully rubbed in.

3 Stir in any additional flavorings, if using, such as ground nuts, cheese, or sugar for sweet pastry.

4 Add the liquid all at once and use your fingers to bring the dough together. Turn the dough out onto a lightly floured counter and knead very lightly. Ideally, the dough should be wrapped in foil or plastic wrap and chilled in the refrigerator for 30 minutes to allow the dough to "relax," which helps to prevent it from shrinking when it is baked.

5 Roll out the dough on a lightly floured counter. Rolling should be carried out in short, sharp strokes, with a light, even pressure in a forward movement only. Turn the dough as you roll.

6 Use as required, then allow the dough to relax again in a cool place for 15-30 minutes before baking. This is especially important if you have not previously relaxed the dough.

7 Bake in a hot oven for 15-20 minutes until set. The temperature may then be reduced.

Short-crust pastry can be made in a food processor, which helps keep it cooler than warm hands. Put the flour and fat in the processor and process until the mixture resembles fine bread crumbs. The liquid can then be added to the machine, processing until the dough comes together. Alternatively, for greater control, tip the flour and fat mixture into a bowl and add the liquid by hand.

The proportion of fat to flour can be increased, or eggs added to produce richer pastries such as pâté sucrée. Because of the increased fat content, these pastries can be more difficult to handle. In some cases, the fat content is so high that additional liquid is not needed to bring the dough together. Rolling out these extra-rich pastries can be made easier by rolling the dough between two sheets of plastic wrap. Additional ingredients such as ground nuts, lemon rind, sugar, or spices can be added for flavor.

BAKING BLIND

When used to line a pan, short-crust pastry is often precooked to set the dough before the filling is added.

The term used to describe this is "baking blind."

1 Line the pan with the rolled-out dough and prick the base with a fork.

2 Chill for about 30 minutes in the refrigerator or 10 minutes in the freezer (you can also bake pastry shells blind from frozen).

3 Line the pastry shell with a sheet of nonstick parchment paper, waxed paper, or foil and fill with purpose-made ceramic or metal baking beans or dried beans or rice. These baking beans

help to conduct heat and cook the dough, as well as preventing the dough from puffing up in the center.

4 Bake for 10 minutes, then remove the paper and beans and bake for an additional 10 minutes until the pastry is just golden.

5 Remove from the oven and brush a little beaten egg or egg white over the base to seal (the heat of the pastry will cook the egg).

PUFF PASTRY

Both flaky and puff pastry are more difficult to make and very time consuming, but their richness, especially in the case of puff pastry, gives them a superior flavor. More experienced bakers will enjoy the challenge of making these pastries as well as the end results. Puff pastry has the highest proportion of fat to flour (equal proportions) and is therefore the most difficult to handle. The principle behind the pastry is to create many layers of dough and butter by folding and turning the two together. For an evenly layered pastry, it is important that you always roll it to the same thickness and that the edges are very straight and even.

scant 2¹/₂ cups all-purpose flour

³/₄ cup unsalted butter

8 tbsp cold water

BASIC METHOD

1 Sift the flour into a bowl and rub in one-quarter of the butter.

2 Add the water and use your fingers to bring the dough together. Knead briefly to form a smooth dough. Put in a plastic bag and chill in the refrigerator for 30 minutes.

3 Roll out the remaining butter between 2 sheets of plastic wrap to form a block about ¹/₂ inch/1 cm thick.

4 Roll out the dough to a square about 4 times the size of the block of butter.

5 Put the block of butter in the center of the dough and fold over the corners of the dough to completely enclose the butter.

6 Roll out the dough into a rectangle 3 times as long as it is wide.

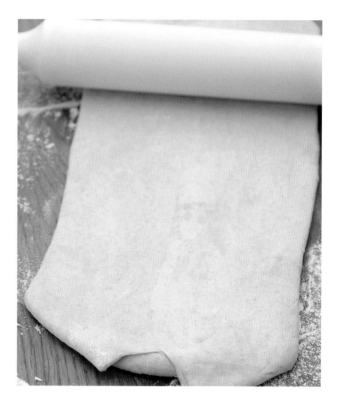

7 Fold one-third of the dough over to cover the middle third, then fold the remainder over the top.

8 Give the dough a half turn, roll out to form another rectangle and fold again as before. Repeat the initial rolling and folding 6 times in total, chilling the dough frequently between rolling.

9 Let relax for a final 30 minutes, then use as required. Trim the folded edges of the dough before using to assist the rising. Bake in a hot oven. The pastry should rise 6–8 times its original height.

FLAKY (PHYLLO) PASTRY

This uses a slightly lower proportion of fat to flour—two-thirds to three-quarters fat to flour—and the fat is added in stages. It is advisable to use a white bread flour for flaky pastry. After the initial fat has been added, the dough is kneaded to develop the elasticity of the gluten, resulting in an elastic dough that will rise easily. A little lemon juice is added to help develop the gluten and counteract the richness of the pastry. The dough must be allowed to relax before being baked. Once cooked, the pastry does not keep long unless frozen, although the uncooked dough can be stored in the refrigerator for up to 48 hours. Uncooked dough can also be sealed and frozen for up to four months.

scant 1⁵⁄₈ cups all-purpose flour
³⁄₄ cup unsalted butter
6–7 tbsp cold milk or water

BASIC METHOD

1 Sift the flour into a bowl and rub in one-quarter of the fat.

2 Add the water and use your fingers to bring the mixture together. Knead briefly to form a smooth dough.

3 Roll out the dough into a rectangle 3 times as long as it is wide.

4 Dot one-third of the remaining fat over two-thirds of the dough in rough lumps. Fold the uncovered dough over to cover half the fatted dough, then fold the remaining third over the top.

5 Seal the edges of the dough by pressing down with a rolling pin.

6 Give the dough a half turn, roll out to form another rectangle and repeat steps 4 and 5 twice more until all the fat has been used. Put the dough in a plastic bag and chill in the refrigerator for 30 minutes.

7 Roll and fold the dough 3 more times as before, but without the addition of fat. Let relax for a final 30 minutes, then use as required. Trim the folded edges of the dough before using to assist the rising. Bake in a hot oven.

ROUGH PUFF

This pastry is relatively easy to make and produces a fabulous light, flaky pastry. It can be a little sticky to handle to begin with. It has a similar fat content to flaky pastry.

scant 1⁵/₈ cups all-purpose flour
³/₄ cup unsalted butter
6-7 tbsp cold milk or water

BASIC METHOD

1 Sift the four into a bowl and add the fat cut into small squares or lumps.

2 Add the water and use your fingers to bring the dough together. Knead very lightly.

3 Roll and fold the dough as for puff pastry.

4 Chill for 30 minutes before using and bake in a hot oven.

SUET CRUST PASTRY

Suet crust pastry is a filling, homely kind of pastry. Self-rising flour or all-purpose flour and baking powder is used to make this.

scant 1⁵/₈ cups all-purpose flour
5 oz/150 g suet (before shredding)
2 tsp baking powder
²/₃ cup cold water

BASIC METHOD

1 Sift the flour into a bowl.

2 Shred, and stir in the suet and baking powder.

3 Add enough water to form an elastic dough.

4 Only roll out the dough once to prevent producing a hard pastry.

COVERING A PIE

This is the basic method for making a single crust to cover a savory or sweet pie filling. You can then add decorative details and a glaze to enhance the appearance of the pie.

1 Roll out the pie dough to about 2 inches/ 5 cm larger all round than the top of the dish.

2 Cut a strip about 1 inch/2.5 cm wide from the edge of the dough.

3 Moisten the edge of the dish and stick the dough strip to the dish.

4 Fill the pie and dampen the dough strip with a little water.

5 Using a rolling pin, carefully lift the dough over the pie. Press the edge down to seal.

6 Using a sharp knife, trim the edge and make a small hole in the center of the pie to allow the steam to escape.

HOT WATERCRUST PASTRY

This traditional type of pastry is used for raised pies, such as pork or game pies. It is the exception to one of the basic rules of pastry making in that its success depends on the warmth of the utensils and flour throughout the making and shaping. If it becomes too cold, it will be difficult to handle.

scant 1 cup all-purpose flour
3 oz/85 g shortening
5 tbsp water

BASIC METHOD

1 Sift the flour into a bowl and make a well in the center.

2 Put the shortening and water in a pan and heat until the fat melts, then bring to a boil. Immediately add to the well in the flour and mix with a spoon to form a dough, then knead the dough.

3 The dough should be shaped while still warm and cooked in a hot oven.

CHOUX PASTRY

This is a rich, soft pastry that relies predominately on its high water content, which becomes very hot during cooking to form a hollow pastry shell.

scant $5/8$ cup white bread flour
4 tbsp unsalted butter
$2/3$ cup water
2 eggs

BASIC METHOD

1 Sift the flour.

2 Put the butter and water in a pan and heat until the fat melts.

3 Add the flour to the pan all at once and beat with a wooden spoon until the mixture forms a ball around the spoon. Let cool slightly.

4 Gradually beat in the eggs until the dough is smooth and glossy. The more the mixture is beaten, the better the results, as the more air is incorporated.

5 Shape by piping or spoon, as required. Bake in a hot oven.

PASTRY FINISHES

● Use a blunt knife to tap the edge of the pie and knock it up. This also helps to seal the pie fully.

● Press the edge with a floured fork.

● Press one thumb around the edge while you pinch the outside edge between your other thumb and index finger.

● Press a thumb around the edge and draw a knife in a short distance from the edge toward the center of the pie between each thumbprint to create a scalloped edge.

● Decorate the pie by using the pastry trimmings. Cut them into leaves or other shapes, as desired, and stick to the pie crust by moistening slightly.

GLAZES

Glazing the dough will produce a shiny golden surface once baked. You can use milk, beaten egg mixed with a little water, or lightly beaten egg white for glazing. Brush a thin layer over the dough with a pastry brush, but avoid making the dough too wet. For sweet pies, a little superfine sugar can also be sprinkled on top.

COOKIES

Americans use the term "cookie," while the British use the word "biscuit" like the French, which means "twice baked." However, in recent times the name "cookie" has been widely adopted outside of the United States along with the spread in popularity of the traditionally American-style chunky variety, such as the chocolate chip cookie. But whatever you call them and whether melt-in-the-mouth crumbly or deliciously chewy, homemade cookies are always a real treat. The range and variety is almost endless— spicy, fruity, nutty, wafer-thin, or thick bars, to mention but a few kinds. You can find a cookie that is perfect for any occasion, be it a decadent coffee morning, hearty afternoon tea, an elegant dinner, or a packed lunch on the run.

Because cookies cook quickly, you will need to keep a close eye on the baking until you become more experienced in gauging the exact cooking time easily. For most cookies, let cool on the cookie sheet for a few minutes before transferring to a cooling rack to cool completely. Many cookies are very soft when they come out of the oven but crisp on cooling, so remember to remove them from the pan before they become completely cold or they may stick.

Store in an airtight container to retain freshness and crispness. Most cookies also freeze well—simply thaw at room temperature.

ROLLED AND MOLDED COOKIES

Here the cookie dough is rolled out and cut out or shaped into logs, balls, or crescents. Take care not to add too much extra flour when rolling and shaping, as this will alter the careful balance of the ingredients. If a dough is very soft, you may find it easier to roll out between two sheets of plastic wrap. Try to avoid re-rolling too many times, or the cookies may become tough.

DROP COOKIES

These are the quickest and easiest to make. They are often made by the creaming method, where the fat and sugar are beaten together, then the flour and any additional flavorings such as nuts or chocolate chips are added. The mixture is then beaten just enough to bring all the ingredients together in a soft dough, which can then be dropped onto the cookie sheet from spoons. Always place well spaced apart on the cookie sheet, as the cookies will spread during baking.

PIPED COOKIES

Some cookies are piped from a plain or fluted pastry tip to produce a decorative effect. The consistency of the cookie dough needs to be just right—too stiff and the dough will be hard to pipe; too soft and the cookies will lose their shape when baked.

WAFERS

Some classic cookies are very thin and crisp. The mixture is very soft (that of a batter) and is spooned onto a cookie sheet and spread out to form a circle. These are probably the hardest cookies to bake, as they bake very rapidly. They are sometimes shaped into rolls or curled. In this case, you need to work fast, only baking a couple at a time, as they need to be shaped while still warm.

SLICED COOKIES

The dough in this instance is firm and can be shaped into a log. The individual cookies are then sliced at the desired thickness. The uncooked cookie dough can be stored in the refrigerator for several days and a few cookies cut and baked from the log as desired. This is an ideal way of making freshly baked cookies every day.

BREADS AND YEAST COOKING

There are so many different kinds of homemade bread that they can easily fill a book in themselves. Many, like soda bread, plain white bread, malt bread, and rolls are great basics, but once mastered, the temptation to move on to making delicious flavored breads is hard to resist. Not all breads rely on yeast as a raising agent and you will find a selection of breads made without yeast in this book. Sweet yeast breads and buns are delicious for high tea, breakfast, or a snack.

Yeast cooking is not particularly difficult and the results are most rewarding. In contrast to working with pie dough, a warm kitchen will help you on the way. Also, there is no need for the caution in handling that pie dough requires–a firm hand is perfect for kneading the dough to develop the gluten content of the bread, which gives it its unique texture. Of course, you do need to allow more time to produce yeasted products, but for the most part they can be left alone to rise and prove while you are free to do other things.

Most yeasted breads and bakes freeze well, so when time is plentiful, they are ideal for batch baking. The frozen bakes can be thawed at room temperature and refreshed in a hot oven for 5 minutes to warm through before serving.

TYPES OF YEAST

Yeast is the raising agent most frequently used for breads. It is a living organism that, when active, creates carbon dioxide. Small bubbles of carbon dioxide then become trapped within the structure of the dough, giving bread its characteristic structure.

There are two main types of bread yeasts available: fresh and dried.

FRESH YEAST

This can be purchased from health food stores and some bakeries. It has a creamy color and is moist and firm. Fresh yeast is usually dissolved in the liquid and allowed a preliminary fermentation before being added to the remaining ingredients. It will only keep for a few days in the refrigerator, but can be frozen for up to three months.

GLUTEN

Gluten is formed by a combination of two proteins, gliadin and glutenin, which are found in wheat flour. Strong flours have a higher proportion of these proteins than soft flour. When these proteins are hydrated, they bond with each other, creating a large protein called gluten that gives the bread its structure. The longer the dough is kneaded, the stronger the gluten becomes and the better texture the bread has. It is possible to knead the dough so much that it becomes too warm and the gluten begins to break down, but this is very unlikely to happen if kneading by hand. If you choose to knead in a mixer, knead for short bursts, allowing a few seconds each time for the dough to cool slightly.

DRIED YEAST

This is available in two forms. Regular dried yeast requires a preliminary fermentation and is activated by mixing with a little liquid and sugar or flour. Active dry yeast, fast-action dried yeast, and instant dried yeast are just different names for yeast that does not require this preliminary fermentation and is simply stirred into the flour before the liquid is added. The first rising and knocking back can also be eliminated if time is short. Dried yeast has a longer shelf life than fresh yeast and does not need to be refrigerated.

EFFECTS OF TEMPERATURE ON YEAST

Yeast works quickest in warm temperatures, so it is generally recommended that the dough is left in a warm place to rise. However, yeast does not stop working at lower temperatures—it simply slows down. Therefore, dough can be made, shaped, and then left to rise overnight in a refrigerator. Allow the dough to return to room temperature before baking. Yeast that is left to work in slower conditions produces a loaf that many people regard as having more flavor and character.

EFFECTS OF OTHER INGREDIENTS ON YEAST ACTION

A basic loaf consists of just flour, yeast, salt, and water, but some breads as well as buns, cakes, and even pastries are made with yeast doughs that have been enriched with other ingredients such as butter, sugar, and eggs. Additional ingredients may contribute to the rising, give added color to the crumb and crust, and may also improve the keeping qualities. However, all these additional ingredients will have an effect on the action of yeast.

● Sugar in small amounts speeds up the action of yeast, but in larger quantities—above 2 oz/55 g per 1 lb/450 g—it will retard the action of yeast.

● Fat in proportions above 1 oz/25 g per 1 lb/450 g will retard the action of yeast.

● Eggs, because of their fat content, may slow the action of yeast, but they also have the ability to retain air in the mixture, so often help to produce a lighter texture.

To overcome any adverse effects of these added ingredients:

● Allow additional time for the rising—2 hours or more is not unusual.

● Make the dough in two parts, with the additional ingredients added after an initial rising.

● Extra yeast may be added.

A NOTE ABOUT SALT

Salt is an essential ingredient in bread making, as it not only adds flavor but also strengthens the gluten structure, and helps control the growth of yeast. Too little and the result will be a poor gluten structure; too much and the salt will inhibit the action of the yeast. Both will result in a loaf of poor volume and flavor. For this reason, it is important not to vary the amount of salt in a recipe, even if you are trying to reduce your salt intake, as this will adversely affect the finished product.

YEAST BREADS

BASIC METHOD

The method used is basically the same for all yeast breads, although individual steps may vary according to the recipe.

$1^{1}/_{2}$ lb/675 g white bread flour
2 tbsp olive oil or 2 tbsp butter
2 tsp salt
2 tsp active dry yeast
about 2 cups lukewarm water

1 Sift the flour and salt into a large bowl. Stir in the active dry yeast, and make a well in the center. Pour in the liquid and mix to a soft, slightly sticky dough.

2 Turn out the dough onto a lightly floured counter and begin kneading by folding the dough over on top of itself and pushing away with the heal of your hand—do not be afraid to be quite forceful. Keep kneading, giving the dough a quarter turn as you do so, for 10 minutes, or until the dough is very

smooth and elastic and no longer sticky. Alternatively, knead the dough in an electric mixer fitted with a dough hook for 6-8 minutes.

3 Form the dough into a ball and put in a lightly oiled bowl. Rub a little oil over the surface of the dough to prevent it drying out and cover loosely with plastic wrap or slide the bowl inside a clean plastic carrier bag. Let rise in a warm place for 1 hour, or until doubled in size.

4 When the dough has increased to double its original size, turn out onto a lightly floured work counter and lightly knead again for a few minutes. This is called "knocking back," as some of the air that has been incorporated into the dough is knocked out and the dough shrinks in size. This ensures that the bread has a more even texture, as any large air pockets are removed at this stage.

5 Shape the dough as required and place in a lightly greased loaf pan. The dough should half-fill the pan.

6 Cover loosely again and let rise (prove) for a second time until doubled in size.

7 Bake in a hot oven. To test if the bread is cooked, turn out of the pan and tap the base. The loaf should sound hollow. Let cool on a cooling rack.

YEAST-FREE BREADS

Some breads do not contain yeast. These breads use another method to leaven the bread (make the bread rise) or are unleavened. Sometimes called quick breads, soda bread and cornbread fall into the former category. Baking soda or baking powder is added to the dough. These produce carbon dioxide, a process that begins as soon as the dough is mixed, so the bread must be baked immediately. The dough should be soft and sticky, and in some cases is more like a thick batter. Quick breads have a soft, crumbly texture and some are best served warm. Most are best eaten the day they are made.

Unleavened breads are sometimes called flat breads. Some flat breads, such as naan and pita bread are in fact leavened with yeast but unleavened dough can also be used. Flat breads are among the oldest breads. Evidence has been found that they were cooked on stones in Neolithic times. Paratha, tortillas and chapatis are all examples of yeast-free flat breads. In the modern home, they can be cooked on a griddle or in a heavy-bottom skillet. Flat breads can be topped like pizza and focaccia, stuffed like pita bread, filled with beans and rice and rolled like chapatis or tortillas, or used for dipping like poppadums from India.

BREAD MACHINES

You can make bread with the minimum of fuss and effort by using a bread machine. Once all the ingredients have been weighed and added to the pan, the machine can be left to do the hard work and a few hours later you have a freshly baked loaf. Although some of the fun of making bread is removed, it is nevertheless a very convenient way of producing freshly baked, warm bread, and as most machines have a timer, you can set it so that you can enjoy it when you wake up in the morning. Always follow the manufacturer's instructions, as quantities of ingredients and methods may vary.

WHAT WENT WRONG?

Accurate measuring and careful following of the recipe should ensure success. However, when things do go wrong, there is often a simple reason, and if you identify the cause, the mistake can be avoided in the future. Baking does not have to be absolutely perfect every time. Little imperfections and variations add to the charm of home baking and distinguish the end results from the rather dull, characterless mass-produced baked goods.

CAKES

SUNK IN THE MIDDLE
- Cake slightly undercooked
- Oven door opened too early
- Batter too wet
- Overbeating of the fat and sugar
- Too much raising agent
- Oven temperature too low

UNEVEN RISE
- Batter not spread evenly
- Flour not folded in evenly (whisked sponges)
- Oven not properly preheated
- Oven or oven shelves not level

PEAKED OR CRACKED TOP
- Baking in too hot an oven so that the crust cooks too quickly–as the cake's center cooks and rises, it is forced to push through the cooked crust, causing it to crack
- Too much batter in the pan
- Too much raising agent
- Batter too wet or too dry
- Cooking too near the top of the oven (again cooking the crust too quickly)

CRUST TOO PALE
- Cake cooked too low in the oven
- Oven overloaded
- Oven temperature too low

CRUST TOO DARK
- Cake cooked too near the top of the oven
- Oven temperature too high
- Pan too large
- Baked too long
- Cake not protected with paper (rich fruit cake)

SPECKLED TOP
- Insufficient beating of fat and sugar
- Granulated or raw brown sugar used

CRACKED JELLY ROLL
- Batter too dry
- Too much batter in pan
- Overcooked
- Rolled up when cold

SUNKEN FRUIT
- Batter too wet to support the fruit
- Fruit too large and heavy
- Fruit is wet
- Oven temperature too low
- Oven door opened during cooking

SHORT-CRUST PASTRY

DIFFICULT TO ROLL
- Too dry

- Self-rising flour used instead of all-purpose flour
- Too much fat
- Overmixed

EXCESSIVE SHRINKING

- Overhandling
- Dough stretched when rolling
- Not allowing dough to rest before baking

SOGGY PASTRY

- Not fully cooked
- Too much liquid
- Pie cover placed over hot filling
- No vent for steam to escape (pies)
- Filling poured into pastry shell that has cracks or holes in (tarts and flans)–seal with a little beaten egg after baking blind

HARD OR TOUGH PASTRY

- Overhandling
- Too little fat
- Too much liquid
- Oven temperature too low

TARTS WITH RISEN CENTER OR COLLAPSED SIDES

- Self-rising flour used instead of all-purpose flour
- Pie dough not pricked before baking
- Not weighted with baking beans during blind baking

BLISTERED CRUST

- Water not evenly mixed in
- Fat not properly rubbed in

CHOUX PASTRY
PASTE TOO THIN

- Water not boiled when flour added
- Inaccurate number of eggs

PASTE TOO THICK

- Liquid boiled for too long
- Wrong egg size

CLOSE, HEAVY TEXTURE

- Insufficient beating
- Oven temperature too low

BADLY CRACKED

- Oven temperature too high

BREAD
INSUFFICIENT RISING

- Too little yeast
- Too little sugar
- Too much salt
- Yeast out of date
- Insufficient time proving (for rich yeast mixture)
- Proving at too low a temperature

BREAD RISEN TOO MUCH

- Too much yeast
- Too little salt

SUNK IN THE CENTER

- Too much liquid
- Too little salt
- Too much yeast
- Overproving

CENTER SOGGY

- Too much of the wet ingredients/water
- Oven temperature too high

DAMP CRUST

- Left in the pan too long after baking
- Wrapped while warm

CRUST TOO DARK

- Too much sugar
- Cooked too long or at too high a temperature

DENSE TEXTURE

- Not enough liquid
- Soft flour used
- Insufficient kneading
- Too much salt
- Liquid too hot (kills the yeast)
- Grains without sufficient gluten used

COARSE, OPEN TEXTURE

- Too much liquid
- Overproving
- Oven temperature too low

FLAT TOP

- Flour too soft
- Dough too wet

GLOSSARY OF BAKING TERMS

BAIN-MARIE

This is a water bath. The baking pan or dish is placed in another containing hot water, resulting in very gentle cooking.

BAKE BLIND

The term given to the process of par-baking pastry shells.

BAKING BEANS

Used to weight pie dough down while baking blind. Baking beans can be purpose-made ceramic or metal beans, or dried beans or rice. All can be reused.

BEAT

Method of incorporating air into ingredients, or combining or softening an ingredient with a spoon, whisk, or fork.

CREAMING

The process of beating sugar and fat together until the mixture is creamy in both color and texture.

DOUGH

A mixture of flour and liquids, dough can be described as either soft or firm, depending on its stiffness.

DREDGE

Sprinkle generously.

DUST

Sprinkle lightly.

FERMENTATION

A term used to describe the chemical action produced by yeast as it converts sugars in the flour to carbon dioxide and alcohol (which evaporates during baking).

FOLDING IN

The term used to describe carefully incorporating flour into a mixture using a cutting and folding-over movement.

GLAZE

A thin, shiny coating that may be of egg, egg white, milk, water, or jelly.

GLUTEN

Proteins in flour that can be developed by kneading in the form of a dough which makes the dough elastic.

KNEAD

Working together of a dough with the hands. For pastry, scones, and cookies, light kneading is required. For bread, heavy, prolonged kneading is required to develop the gluten.

KNOCK BACK

To knead dough for a second time after the first rising. This helps to ensure an even texture.

PIPING

The process of pushing a mixture through a bag fitted with a piping tip to shape. Some cookies and choux pastry can be piped to shape. Piping is also used to shape frosting to decorate cakes or cookies.

PROVE

To let bread rise a second time after knocking back and shaping it.

RUB IN

Rub fat into flour with the fingertips until evenly distributed.

SIFT

To shake dry ingredients through a sifter. Sifting flour helps to incorporate air.

SYRUP

A concentrated solution of sugar in water.

UNLEAVENED

A term used for breads that do not use a raising agent.

WHIP

The same as whisk, but is usually used in relation to cream and creamy mixtures.

WHISK

To beat ingredients rapidly to incorporate air into them.

cookies

There's a cookie for every occasion. Equally at home on a fine china plate as packed into a plastic lunchbox, the beauty of the cookie is that it can be dressed up or down simply depending on its shape, decoration, and ingredients. Whether melt-in-the-mouth soft or deliciously chewy, the different varieties are endless. Choose from spicy, nutty, thin, or thick bars, not to mention the many different shapes found in this chapter. As well as the regular "cut" cookies there are sliced cookies, piped cookies, molded cookies, shaped cookies, dropped cookies, and wafer cookies. But whatever type of cookie you go for, do not forget to check them as they bake to avoid overcooking!

MAKES 24

1 cup all-purpose flour, plus extra
   for dusting

1¹/₂ tsp ground allspice

¹/₂ tsp ground ginger

pinch of salt

¹/₂ tsp baking soda

8 tbsp butter or margarine, plus extra
   for greasing

¹/₂ cup packed light brown sugar

2 small eggs

1 tsp unsweetened cocoa

¹/₂ tsp Kahlúa

TO SERVE

¹/₂ cup heavy cream or
   sour cream

12 fresh mint sprigs

¹/₄ cup hazelnuts, toasted and
   coarsely chopped

MELTING HEARTS

Sift the flour, allspice, ginger, salt, and baking soda together into a large bowl. Cream the butter and sugar together in a separate bowl until pale and fluffy, then beat in the eggs. Gradually add the cocoa, Kahlúa, and flour mixture and continue beating until smooth. Cover with plastic wrap and let chill in the refrigerator for at least 8 hours or overnight if possible.

When ready to bake, preheat the oven to 350°F/180°C and grease a cookie sheet. Roll out the dough on a lightly floured counter into a rectangle about ¹/₈ inch/3 mm thick, then cut out 24 heart shapes using a cookie cutter or a sharp knife. Transfer to the prepared cookie sheet. Bake in the preheated oven for 15 minutes, or until golden brown.

Transfer to a cooling rack, and let cool. When cool, serve with heavy cream or sour cream topped with mint sprigs. Sprinkle over the hazelnuts.

Serve these little heart-shaped cookies with a cup of coffee, or to round off a romantic Valentine's Day dinner.

HAZELNUT BITES

Preheat the oven to 350°F/180°C. Grease a large cookie sheet or sheets. Cream the butter and sugar together in a bowl until pale and fluffy. Add the egg and almond extract and beat well. Sift the flour, baking powder, and salt together into a separate bowl, then beat in the creamed mixture. Stir in the oats, chocolate chips, and half the nuts.

Drop 24 teaspoonfuls of the dough onto the prepared cookie sheet or sheets and flatten with a rolling pin. Bake in the preheated oven for 10 minutes, or until golden brown.

Transfer to a cooling rack and let cool completely. Melt the chocolate pieces in a heatproof bowl set over a pan of barely simmering water. Cover the tops of the cookies with the melted chocolate, then top with a sprinkling of the remaining hazelnuts. Let set on waxed paper before serving. Store the cookies in an airtight container in the refrigerator.

MAKES 24

8 tbsp butter, plus extra
  for greasing
scant 3/4 cup packed raw brown sugar
1 egg
1 tbsp almond extract
1 cup all-purpose flour
3/4 tsp baking powder
pinch of salt
1 cup rolled oats
1/2 cup semisweet chocolate chips
scant 3/4 cup hazelnuts, toasted
  and chopped
10 1/2 oz/300 g semisweet chocolate
  pieces

Toasted hazelnuts and chocolate partner each other very successfully. Use milk or white chocolate if preferred.

CANDIED FRUIT COOKIES

A flavorful addition to the cookie jar, these cookies are delicious at any time of the day. Store for up to a week.

MAKES 20

2 egg whites

scant 1⁵/₈ cups blanched almonds, finely ground

scant ³/₄ cup superfine sugar

1 tsp finely grated orange rind

¹/₂ tsp ground cinnamon

2 tbsp candied fruit, plus extra to decorate

raw brown sugar, for sprinkling

Preheat the oven to 350°F/180°C. Line 2 large cookie sheets with nonstick parchment paper.

Beat the egg whites in a large bowl until stiff. Using a knife, gently fold in the ground almonds, superfine sugar, orange rind, cinnamon, and fruit until smooth.

Transfer the mixture to a pastry bag fitted with a large tip (at least ¹/₂ inch/1 cm in diameter). Pipe 20 x 3-inch/7.5-cm circles onto the parchment paper, spaced well apart to allow for spreading. Sprinkle with the raw brown sugar.

Bake in the preheated oven for 20 minutes, or until light brown.

Transfer to a cooling rack. Decorate with candied fruit and let cool completely before serving.

COFFEE WHOLE WHEAT BAKES

Preheat the oven to 375°F/190°C. Grease a large cookie sheet, or sheets. Cream the butter and sugar together in a bowl until pale and fluffy. Add the egg and beat well.

Sift the white flour, baking soda, and salt together into a separate bowl, then stir in the whole wheat flour and bran. Beat in the creamed mixture, then stir in the chocolate chips, oats, coffee, and hazelnuts. Mix well, using an electric mixer if preferred.

Drop 24 rounded tablespoonfuls of the dough onto the prepared cookie sheet, spaced well apart to allow for spreading.

Alternatively, with lightly floured hands, break off pieces of the dough and roll into balls (about 1 oz/25 g each), put on the cookie sheet, and flatten with the back of a teaspoon.

Bake the cookies in the preheated oven for 16–18 minutes, or until golden brown.

Transfer to a cooling rack and let cool before serving.

MAKES 24

3/4 cup butter or margarine, plus
    extra for greasing

1 cup packed light brown sugar

1 egg

1/2 cup all-purpose flour, plus extra
    for dusting

1 tsp baking soda

pinch of salt

scant 1/2 cup whole wheat flour

1 tbsp bran

1 1/3 cups semisweet chocolate chips

generous 1 cup rolled oats

1 tbsp cold strong black coffee

scant 3/4 cup hazelnuts, toasted and
    coarsely chopped

These delicious, dark cookies, flavored with coffee and toasted
chopped hazelnuts, are perfect served with coffee.

MAKES 20

1 lb/450 g all-purpose flour, plus extra
   for dusting

2 tsp ground ginger

1 tsp ground allspice

2 tsp baking soda

8 tbsp butter, plus extra
   for greasing

generous $^1/_3$ cup corn syrup

generous $^1/_2$ cup packed light
   brown sugar

1 egg, beaten

TO DECORATE

currants

candied cherries

$^3/_4$ cup confectioners' sugar

3-4 tsp water

GINGERBREAD PEOPLE

Preheat the oven to 325°F/160°C.
Grease 3 large cookie sheets. Sift
the flour, ginger, allspice, and
baking soda together into a large
bowl. Put the butter, syrup, and
brown sugar in a pan over low
heat and stir until melted. Pour
onto the flour mixture and add

the egg. Mix together to make a dough. The dough will be sticky to start
with, but will become firmer as it cools.

Roll out the dough on a lightly floured counter to about $^1/_8$ inch/3 mm
thick, then cut out about 20 gingerbread people using a cookie cutter.
Transfer to the prepared cookie sheets. Decorate with currants for eyes
and pieces of cherry for mouths.

Bake the cookies in the preheated oven for 15-20 minutes, or until
firm and lightly browned.

Let cool on the cookie sheets for a few minutes, then transfer to
cooling racks and let cool completely. Mix the confectioners' sugar with
the water in a small bowl to a thick consistency. Transfer the frosting to
a small plastic bag and cut a tiny hole in one corner. Use to pipe buttons
or bows onto the cookies.

This is a favorite with children, who love to make the gingerbread shapes.
The recipe makes a pliable dough that is very easy to handle.

At Christmas, cut out star and bell shapes. When the cookies come out of the oven,
gently pierce a hole in each one with a skewer. Thread ribbons through and
hang on the Christmas tree.

OATMEAL PECAN BISCUITS

Preheat the oven to 350°F/180°C. Grease 2 cookie sheets. Cream the butter and sugar together in a bowl until pale and fluffy. Gradually beat in the egg, then stir in the nuts.

Sift the flour and baking powder together into the creamed mixture and add the oats. Stir together until well combined. Drop 15 dessertspoonfuls of the dough onto the prepared cookie sheets, spaced well apart to allow for spreading.

Bake in the preheated oven for 15 minutes, or until pale golden. Let cool on the cookie sheets for 2 minutes, then transfer to cooling racks and let cool completely.

MAKES 15

8 tbsp butter, softened,
   plus extra for greasing
generous 3/8 cup packed brown sugar
1 egg, beaten
generous 3/8 cup pecans, chopped
scant 5/8 cup all-purpose flour
1/2 tsp baking powder
1/3 cup rolled oats

These light, crisp biscuits are delicious just as they are, but they also taste exceptionally good served with cheese.

For a slightly different taste, substitute other chopped nuts for the pecans, such as walnuts or hazelnuts.

To save a lot of hard work, cream the butter and sugar together with a hand-held electric whisk. Alternatively, use a food processor.

ORANGE HORNS

It is much easier to shape these cookies into horn shapes while they are still warm from the oven. Let them cool before serving.

MAKES 30

8 tbsp butter or margarine, plus extra
    for greasing

generous $5/8$ cup packed brown sugar

pinch of salt

1 egg white, lightly beaten

$1/2$ tsp baking powder

3 oz/85 g oatmeal

1 cup finely chopped Brazil nuts or
    hazelnuts

1 tbsp milk

grated rind of 1 orange

1 tsp orange juice

Preheat the oven to 325°F/160°C. Lightly grease a large cookie sheet.

Cream the butter and sugar together in a bowl until pale and fluffy. Add the remaining ingredients and mix thoroughly.

Drop 30 rounded teaspoonfuls of the dough onto the prepared cookie sheet and flatten into small circles using the bottom of a glass.

Bake in the preheated oven for 7 minutes.

Let cool slightly, then lay each cookie in turn on a rolling pin to help start the desired curve, completing the horn shape by hand, while the cookie is still warm.

Transfer to a cooling rack and let cool completely before serving.

PEANUT BUTTER COOKIES

MAKES 20

8 tbsp butter, softened, plus extra
    for greasing

generous $1/3$ cup crunchy peanut
    butter

generous $1^1/8$ cups granulated sugar

1 egg, lightly beaten

generous 1 cup all-purpose flour, plus
    extra for dusting

$1/2$ tsp baking powder

pinch of salt

$1/2$ cup chopped unsalted peanuts

For extra crunch and a sparkling
appearance, sprinkle the cookies
with raw brown sugar before baking.

Beat the butter and peanut butter together in a large bowl. Gradually add the sugar and beat well.

Add the egg, a little at a time, beating well after each addition, until thoroughly combined.

Sift the flour, baking powder, and salt together into the mixture. Add the peanuts and mix together to form a soft dough. Wrap in plastic wrap and let chill in the refrigerator for 30 minutes.

When ready to bake, preheat the oven to 350°F/180°C. Lightly grease 2 cookie sheets.

Roll the dough into 20 balls on a lightly floured counter. Transfer to the prepared cookie sheets, spaced about 2 inches/5 cm apart to allow for spreading. Flatten slightly with your hand.

Bake in the preheated oven for 15 minutes, or until golden brown.

Transfer to a cooling rack and let cool before serving.

MAKES ABOUT 50

generous $1/3$ cup butter, softened, plus
    extra for greasing

generous $1/2$ cup superfine sugar

grated rind of 1 lemon

1 egg, lightly beaten

4 tbsp lemon juice

generous $2^3/8$ cups all-purpose flour,
    plus extra for dusting

1 tsp baking powder

1 tbsp milk

confectioners' sugar, for dredging

LEMON JUMBLES

Preheat the oven to 325°F/160°C.
Lightly grease several cookie
sheets.

Cream the butter, superfine
sugar, and lemon rind together in
a bowl until pale and fluffy.

Add the beaten egg and lemon
juice, a little at a time, beating
well after each addition, until thoroughly combined.

Sift the flour and baking powder together into the mixture and mix
together. Add the milk and mix to form a firm dough.

Turn out the dough onto a lightly floured counter and divide into
about 50 equal pieces.

Roll each piece into a sausage shape with your hands and twist in the
middle to make an "S" shape. Transfer to the prepared cookie sheets.

Bake in the preheated oven for 15-20 minutes. Transfer to cooling
racks and let cool completely. Dredge the cookies generously with
confectioners' sugar before serving.

If you prefer, shape the dough into other shapes—letters of the alphabet or
geometric shapes—or just form into round cookies.

SUGARED ORANGE DIAMONDS

Wrapped in cellophane and tied with ribbon, these Cointreau-flavored cookies make an attractive gift.

MAKES 24

8 tbsp butter or margarine, plus extra
   for greasing

scant 3/4 cup raw brown sugar

2 tbsp orange juice

1 tbsp Cointreau

generous 2³/8 cups all-purpose flour,
   sifted, plus extra for dusting

scant 1¹/4 cups walnuts,
   coarsely chopped

1 tbsp finely grated orange rind

confectioners' sugar, for dusting

Beat the butter, raw brown sugar, orange juice, and Cointreau together in a bowl until pale and fluffy.

Mix the flour, walnuts, and orange rind together in a separate bowl. Add the creamed mixture and mix until thoroughly combined. Cover with plastic wrap and let chill in the refrigerator for 2 hours.

When ready to bake, preheat the oven to 350°F/180°C. Grease a large cookie sheet.

Roll out the dough on a lightly floured counter into a rectangle about ¹/8 inch/3 mm thick, then use a sharp knife or a cookie cutter to cut out 24 diamond shapes. Transfer the diamond shapes to the prepared cookie sheet. Bake in the preheated oven for 15 minutes, or until golden brown.

Transfer to a cooling rack and let cool. Dust the cookies with confectioners' sugar before serving.

MAKES 36

6 tbsp butter, diced, plus extra
    for greasing

2 cups all-purpose flour, plus extra
    for dusting

pinch of salt

generous 1⅛ cups superfine sugar

1 egg, beaten

2 tbsp caraway seeds

raw brown sugar, for sprinkling

CARAWAY COOKIES

Preheat the oven to 325°F/160°C. Lightly grease 2 large cookie sheets.

Sift the flour and salt together into a bowl. Rub in the butter with your fingertips until the mixture resembles fine bread crumbs. Stir in the superfine sugar.

Set aside 1 tablespoon of the beaten egg for brushing the cookies. Add the remainder of the egg to the mixture along with the caraway seeds and mix to form a soft dough.

Roll out the dough thinly on a lightly floured counter, then cut out about 36 circles using a 2½-inch/6-cm cookie cutter.

Transfer the circles to the prepared cookie sheets, brush with the reserved egg, and sprinkle with raw brown sugar.

Bake in the preheated oven for 10–15 minutes, or until lightly golden and crisp.

Transfer to a cooling rack and let cool. Store in an airtight container.

The caraway seed is best known for its appearance in rye bread. Here, caraway seeds give these cookies a distinctive flavor.

Caraway seeds have a nutty, delicate anise flavor. If you don't like the taste, replace them with poppy seeds.

CHOCOLATE COOKIES

Preheat the oven to 350°F/180°C. Lightly grease a large cookie sheet.

Using a hand-held electric whisk, beat the egg, sugar, and vanilla extract together in a bowl until thick and pale—the mixture should leave a trail when the whisk is lifted.

Sift the flour, baking powder, and cinnamon together into a separate bowl, then sift again into the egg mixture and fold in gently. Stir in the chocolate, almonds, and pine nuts.

Turn out the dough on a lightly floured counter and shape into a flat log, measuring 9 inches/23 cm long and $3/4$ inch/2 cm wide. Transfer to the prepared cookie sheet.

Bake in the preheated oven for 20-25 minutes, or until golden. Let cool onto the cookie sheet for 5 minutes, or until firm.

Transfer the log to a cutting board. Using a serrated bread knife, cut the log diagonally into 16 slices about $1/2$ inch/1 cm thick and arrange on the cookie sheet. Bake in the oven for an additional 10-15 minutes, turning the biscotti onto the other side halfway through the cooking time to bake evenly.

Let the biscotti cool on the cookie sheet for 5 minutes, then transfer to a cooling rack to cool completely.

MAKES 16

butter, for greasing

1 egg

$1/2$ cup superfine sugar

1 tsp vanilla extract

generous 1 cup all-purpose flour, plus extra for dusting

$1/2$ tsp baking powder

1 tsp ground cinnamon

$13/4$ oz/50 g bittersweet chocolate, coarsely chopped

$1/2$ cup toasted slivered almonds

$3/8$ cup pine nuts

Italian-style dry cookies are a traditional accompaniment to black coffee after dinner, but you may find yourself nibbling them the morning after.

JAMAICAN RUM COOKIES

Dark rum and coconut lend a deliciously exotic flavor to these cookies. They are ideal for serving after dinner with coffee.

MAKES 36

3/4 cup butter or margarine, plus extra for greasing

1/4 cup sesame seeds

generous 1/3 cup chopped mixed nuts

1 cup all-purpose flour

1/4 tsp baking powder

pinch of salt

generous 1 1/3 cups raw brown sugar

1 egg

1 tsp dark rum

2 tbsp coconut flakes, to decorate

Preheat the oven to 350°F/180°C. Lightly grease a large cookie sheet or sheets.

Spread the sesame seeds and chopped nuts out on an ungreased cookie sheet and toast in the preheated oven for 10 minutes, or until slightly browned. Remove from the oven and set aside.

Sift the flour, baking powder, and salt together into a large bowl. Add the sugar, egg, and rum and beat together well.

Drop 36 rounded teaspoonfuls of the dough onto the prepared large cookie sheets, spaced well apart to allow for spreading. Bake in the oven for 8 minutes, or until golden brown.

Transfer to a cooling rack and let cool. Decorate with the coconut flakes and serve.

MILLIONAIRE'S SHORTBREAD

MAKES 9

8 tbsp butter, diced and chilled, plus
   extra for greasing
scant 1⅝ cups all-purpose flour
⅓ cup packed brown sugar, sifted

TOPPING
4 tbsp butter
⅓ cup packed brown sugar
scant 2½ cups condensed milk
5½ oz/150 g milk chocolate

This rich shortbread topped with
caramel and chocolate makes a special
treat for adults and children alike.

Ensure that the caramel layer is
completely cool and set before coating
it with the melted chocolate, otherwise
they will mix together.

Preheat the oven to 375°F/190°C. Lightly grease a 9-inch/23-cm square cake pan.

Sift the flour into a bowl. Rub in the butter with your fingertips until the mixture resembles fine bread crumbs. Add the sugar and work the mixture to form a firm dough. Don't overwork the shortbread, otherwise it will be tough, not crumbly as it should be.

Lightly press the dough into the base of the prepared pan and prick all over with a fork.

Bake in the preheated oven for 20 minutes, or until firm and lightly golden. Let cool in the pan.

To make the topping, put the butter, sugar, and condensed milk in a nonstick pan over low heat and cook, stirring constantly, until the mixture comes to a boil.

Reduce the heat and cook for 4-5 minutes, stirring constantly, until the caramel is pale golden and thick, and coming away from the side of the pan. Pour the topping over the shortbread and let cool.

When the topping is firm, break the chocolate into pieces and melt in a heatproof bowl set over a pan of barely simmering water. Spread over the topping and let set. Cut into 9 squares to serve.

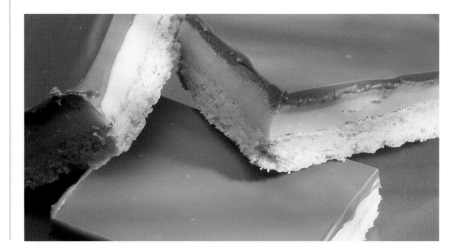

SHORTBREAD TRIANGLES

MAKES 8

8 tbsp butter, diced and chilled, plus
    extra for greasing

scant 1¹/₄ cups flour, plus extra for
    dusting (optional)

pinch of salt

generous ¹/₄ cup superfine sugar

2 tsp golden superfine sugar

Grease a 8-inch/20-cm round fluted cake pan or tart pan. Preheat the oven to 300°F/150°C.

Sift the flour, salt, and superfine sugar together into a bowl. Rub in the butter with your fingertips until the mixture resembles fine bread crumbs. Work the mixture to form a soft dough. Don't overwork the shortbread, otherwise it will be tough, not crumbly as it should be.

Lightly press the dough into the cake pan. If you don't have a fluted pan, roll out the dough on a lightly floured counter. Transfer to a cookie sheet and pinch the edge to form a scalloped pattern.

Mark the dough into 8 equal portions with a knife. Prick all over with a fork and bake in the center of the preheated oven for 45-50 minutes until firm and lightly golden.

Let cool in the pan and dredge with the golden superfine sugar. Cut into portions and transfer to a cooling rack. Store in an airtight container in a cool place.

Shortbread dates back at least to the 16th century. It is ideal for tea-time, coffee in the morning, or as an accompaniment to fruit fools or other soft desserts.

The formula for shortbread is usually one part sugar and two parts butter to three parts flour. The sugar used is often superfine, the butter slightly salted and the flour all-purpose, although sometimes a tablespoon of semolina, rice flour, or corn flour may replace some of the flour to give a different texture.

GINGER-FLAVORED ROLLS

MAKES 36

oil, for oiling

8 tbsp unsalted butter

²/₃ cup corn syrup

generous ¹/₂ cup raw brown sugar

generous ³/₄ cup all-purpose flour

2 tsp ground ginger

2¹/₂ cups stiffly whipped
   heavy cream, to serve

If the rolls become too hard before rolling, pop them back in the oven for a few minutes.

Preheat the oven to 325°F/160°C. Oil a nonstick cookie sheet. Heat the butter, syrup, and sugar in a pan over low heat, stirring occasionally, until melted and combined. Remove from the heat and let cool slightly. Sift the flour and ginger together into the butter mixture and beat until smooth. Spoon 2 teaspoons of the mixture onto the prepared cookie sheet, spaced well apart to allow for spreading. Bake in the preheated oven for 8 minutes until pale golden brown. Keep the remaining mixture warm. Meanwhile, oil the handle of a wooden spoon.

Let stand on the cookie sheet for 1 minute so that the rolls firm up slightly. Remove one with a palette knife and immediately curl it around the handle of the wooden spoon. Once set, carefully slide off the handle and transfer to a cooling rack to cool completely. Repeat with the other roll. Bake the remaining mixture on cool cookie sheets and shape in the same way. Don't be tempted to cook more than 2 rolls at a time, otherwise the circles will set before you have time to shape them. When cool, store in an airtight container.

Spoon the cream into a pastry bag fitted with a star tip. Fill the rolls with cream from both ends. Serve at once or the rolls will soften.

CHRISTMAS COOKIES

MAKES ABOUT 24

2 lb/900 g all-purpose flour, plus
   extra for dusting

1 tbsp baking soda

1 tbsp ground ginger

3 tsp ground allspice

pinch of salt

1 cup butter or margarine, plus extra
   for greasing

1 lb 2 oz/500 g corn syrup

1 cup raw brown sugar

$1/2$ cup water

1 egg

1 tsp brandy

1 tsp very finely grated orange rind

$1/2$ cup confectioners' sugar, plus
   extra for dusting

These festive cookies will quickly
become an annual favorite. Store them
in an airtight container for up
to a week.

Sift the flour, baking soda, ginger, allspice, and salt together into a bowl. Beat the butter, syrup, raw brown sugar, water, egg, and brandy together in a separate bowl until thoroughly combined. Gradually stir in the orange rind, then the flour mixture.

Halve the dough, wrap in plastic wrap, and chill in the refrigerator for at least 4 hours (it will keep for up to 6 days).

When ready to bake, preheat the oven to 350°F/180°C. Grease a cookie sheet. Roll each half of dough into a ball on a lightly floured counter, then roll out to a thickness of $1/8$ inch/3 mm. Cut out about 24 festive shapes such as stars and Christmas trees using cookie cutters or a knife. Transfer to the prepared cookie sheet. Bake in the preheated oven for 10 minutes, or until golden brown. Transfer to a cooling rack and let cool.

When the cookies have cooled, mix the confectioners' sugar with a little water in a small bowl. Drizzle the frosting over some of the cookies and dust the remainder with sifted confectioners' sugar.

CHOCOLATE **CHIP** COOKIES

No chocolate-loving cook's repertoire would be complete without a chocolate chip cookie recipe. This recipe can be used to make several different varieties (see below).

MAKES 18

1¹/2 cups all-purpose flour, sifted

1 tsp baking powder

8 tbsp soft margarine, plus extra for greasing

scant ²/3 cup packed brown sugar

¹/4 cup superfine sugar

¹/2 tsp vanilla extract

1 egg

²/3 cup semisweet chocolate chips

Preheat the oven to 375°F/190°C. Lightly grease 2 cookie sheets. Put all the ingredients in a large bowl and beat well until thoroughly combined.

Drop 18 tablespoonfuls of the dough onto the prepared cookie sheets, spaced well apart to allow for spreading.

Bake in the preheated oven for 10–12 minutes until golden brown. Using a spatula, transfer the cookies to a cooling rack to cool completely before serving.

For Choc and Nut Cookies, add ¹/2 cup chopped hazelnuts to the basic mixture. For Double Choc Cookies, beat in 1¹/2 oz/40 g melted semisweet chocolate. For White Chocolate Chip Cookies, use white chocolate chips instead of the semisweet chocolate chips.

LEMON DROPS

MAKES 24

8 tbsp butter or margarine, plus extra
for greasing

1 cup superfine sugar

2 tbsp lemon juice

1 tbsp finely grated lemon rind

2 tbsp water

scant 1⁵/₈ cups all-purpose flour,
sifted

1 tsp baking soda

¹/₂ tsp cream of tartar

TO DECORATE

confectioners' sugar

candied fruit, finely chopped
(optional)

Preheat the oven to 350°F/180°C. Grease a large cookie sheet. Beat together the butter, superfine sugar, lemon juice, lemon rind, and water.

In a separate bowl, mix together the flour, baking soda, and cream of tartar. Add the butter mixture and blend together well.

Spoon the mixture into a pastry bag fitted with a star-shaped tip. Pipe 24 drops, about the size of a tablespoon, onto the greased cookie sheet, allowing room for the cookies to spread during cooking. Transfer to the preheated oven and bake for 10 minutes, or until the lemon drops are golden brown.

Remove from the oven, then transfer to a cooling rack using a metal spatula and let cool completely. Dust with confectioners' sugar and sprinkle over the candied fruit, if liked. For an alternative topping add a little water to the confectioners' sugar to make a frosting.

Serve these with lemon tea, sweetened with a little honey if liked. They also make a delicious dessert.

small cakes
AND *pastries*

There is nothing so satisfying as creating a tray of little baked delights. This chapter is a celebration of the small cake and its comfortingly indulgent cousin—the pastry. There is a tiny treat for every occasion— from children's birthdays to afternoon snacks, from the classic Cupcake, to the empanada, a sweet-filled pie crust. Whether adorned with silver balls, or shaped into pastry nests, the young and the young at heart will love these tantalizing treats.

CUPCAKES

Preheat the oven to 350°F/180°C. Line 2 muffin pans with 20 muffin paper cases.

Put the water, butter, superfine sugar, and syrup in a pan over low heat and heat, stirring, until the sugar has dissolved. Increase the heat and bring to a boil. Reduce the heat and cook gently for 5 minutes. Remove from the heat and let cool. Put the milk and vanilla extract in a bowl. Add the baking soda and stir to dissolve. Sift the cocoa and flour into a separate bowl and add the syrup mixture. Stir in the milk mixture and beat until smooth.

Carefully spoon the batter into the paper cases to come within two-thirds of the tops. Bake in the preheated oven for 20 minutes, or until well risen and firm to the touch. Transfer to a cooling rack and let cool.

To make the frosting, melt the semisweet chocolate in a small heatproof bowl with half the water and half the butter set over a pan of barely simmering water. Stir until smooth and let stand over the water. Repeat with the white chocolate and remaining water and butter.

Stir half the confectioners' sugar into each bowl and beat until smooth and fudgy. Divide the frosting between the cakes, filling to the tops of the paper cases. Let cool, then place a rose petal on each semisweet chocolate-frosted cake and a violet on each white chocolate-frosted cake. Let set before serving.

These pretty little cakes are light and moist, with a tempting fudgy chocolate topping—perfect for serving at any time of the day.

Instead of the candied flower petals, the cakes could be decorated with chocolate curls or chopped hazelnuts.

MAKES 20

scant 1 cup water

6 tbsp butter

generous 3/8 cup superfine sugar

1 tbsp corn syrup

3 tbsp milk

1 tsp vanilla extract

1 tsp baking soda

2 tbsp unsweetened cocoa

scant 1 5/8 cups all-purpose flour

FROSTNG

1 3/4 oz/50 g semisweet chocolate, broken into pieces

4 tbsp water

3 1/2 tbsp butter

1 3/4 oz/50 g white chocolate, broken into pieces

3 cups confectioners' sugar

TO DECORATE

candied rose petals

candied violets

LAVENDER CUPCAKES

MAKES 12

generous ¹/₂ cup golden superfine
   sugar

8 tbsp butter, softened

2 eggs, beaten

1 tbsp milk

1 tsp finely chopped lavender flowers

¹/₂ tsp vanilla extract

scant 1¹/₄ cups self-rising flour, sifted

1¹/₄ cups confectioners' sugar

TO DECORATE

lavender flowers

silver dragées

Preheat the oven to 400°F/200°C. Line a 12-hole bun pan with cake paper cases.

Cream the superfine sugar and butter together in a bowl until pale and fluffy. Gradually beat in the eggs. Stir in the milk, chopped lavender flowers, and vanilla extract, then gently fold in the flour.

Divide the batter between the paper cases and bake in the preheated oven for 12-15 minutes, or until well risen, golden, and springy to the touch. A few minutes before the cakes are ready, sift the confectioners' sugar into a bowl. Stir in enough water to make a thick frosting.

Transfer the cakes to a cooling rack. Add a blob of frosting to the center of each, allowing it to run across the cake. Decorate with lavender flowers and silver dragées. Serve when cool.

Lavender might seem like an unusual ingredient, but it gives a special fragrance and flavor to these little cakes. Add a little purple food coloring to the frosting to give it a pale lilac color to complement the lavender.

Always make sure that your lavender flowers are suitable to eat and free from any chemical sprays or insecticides.

COCONUT **BARS**

Freshly baked, these chewy bars are always a favorite for after-school snacks and just the thing for tea-time.

The bars are best stored in an airtight container and eaten within a week. They can also be frozen for up to 1 month. Make sure that they are thawed before eating.

MAKES 16

$^7/_8$ cup butter, plus extra

   for greasing

1 cup raw brown sugar

2 tbsp corn syrup

generous 1$^1/_2$ cups porridge oats

$^3/_4$ cup dry unsweetened coconut

2$^3/_4$ oz/75 g candied cherries,

   chopped

Preheat the oven to 325°F/160°C. Grease a 12 x 9 inch/30 x 23 cm cookie sheet.

Put the butter, sugar, and syrup in a large pan over low heat and heat until just melted. Stir in the oats, coconut, and cherries and mix until thoroughly combined.

Spread the mixture evenly into the prepared cookie sheet and press down with the back of a spatula to make a smooth surface.

Bake in the preheated oven for 30 minutes. Let cool on the cookie sheet for 10 minutes. Cut the flapjacks into 16 rectangles using a sharp knife. Carefully transfer the pieces of oat cakes to a cooling rack and let cool completely.

WALNUT PASTRIES

MAKES 12

7 tbsp butter

**3 cups walnut pieces,
finely chopped**

generous 1/4 cup superfine sugar

1 tsp ground cinnamon

1/2 tsp ground cloves

8 oz/225 g phyllo pastry

2/3 cup honey

2 tsp lemon juice

2/3 cup water

These delicious pastries can be
eaten as an afternoon snack or on
special occasions.

Preheat the oven to 425°F/220°C. Put the butter in a pan over low heat and heat until just melted. Use a little to lightly grease a deep 10 x 7-inch/25 x 18-cm roasting pan.

To make the filling, put the walnuts, sugar, cinnamon, and cloves in a bowl and mix together well.

Cut the pastry sheets in half widthwise. Take a sheet of pastry and use to line the pan. Cover the remaining sheets with a damp dish towel. Brush the sheet with a little of the melted butter. Repeat with half the pastry sheets, then sprinkle over the walnut filling. Top with the remaining pastry sheets, brushing each with melted butter and tucking down the edges.

Using a sharp knife, cut the top layers of the pastry into 12 diamond or square shapes.

Bake the pastry in the preheated oven for 10 minutes, then reduce the oven temperature to 350°F/180°C and bake for an additional 20 minutes, or until golden brown.

Just before the pastry is ready, put the honey, lemon juice, and water in a pan over medium heat and simmer for 5 minutes, or until well combined. Set aside.

Remove the pastry from the oven and pour the honey mixture evenly over it. Let cool. To serve, cut along the marked lines again to divide into pieces.

ORANGE AND WALNUT CAKES

Preheat the oven to 350°F/180°C. Sift the flour, baking soda, cinnamon, cloves, nutmeg, and salt together into a bowl. Beat the oil and sugar together in a separate bowl. Add the orange rind and juice, then gradually beat in the flour mixture.

Turn out the dough onto a lightly floured counter and knead for 2–3 minutes until smooth. Oil the cookie sheets.

Break off egg-sized pieces of dough and shape into ovals. Transfer to cookie sheets, spaced well apart to allow for spreading. Using the back of a fork, press the top of each twice to create a criss-cross design.

Bake the cakes in the preheated oven for 20 minutes, or until lightly browned. Transfer to a cooling rack and let cool.

Meanwhile, to make the topping, mix the walnuts and cinnamon together in a small bowl. To make the syrup, put the honey and water in a pan and bring to a boil. Reduce the heat and simmer for 5 minutes. Remove from the heat and add the lemon and orange juices and the brandy.

When the cakes are almost cool, using a slotted spoon, submerge each cake in the hot syrup and leave for about 1 minute. Put on a tray and top each with some of the walnut mixture. Let cool completely before serving.

MAKES ABOUT 18

generous 2 3/4 cups self-rising flour,
 plus extra for dusting

1/2 tsp baking soda

1/2 tsp ground cinnamon

1/4 tsp ground cloves

pinch of freshly grated nutmeg

pinch of salt

2/3 cup olive oil, plus extra for greasing

generous 1/3 cup superfine sugar

finely grated rind and juice of
 1 large orange

TOPPING

1/4 cup walnut pieces,
 finely chopped

1/2 tsp ground cinnamon

SYRUP

1/2 cup honey

1/2 cup water

juice of 1 small lemon

juice of 1 small orange

2 tbsp brandy

These delicately spiced orange-flavored cakes are festive treats. After baking, they are dipped in a hot honey syrup and sprinkled with chopped walnuts. They are intensely sweet, but you can omit the syrup if you don't think it will suit your taste.

MERINGUES

These are just as meringues should be—as light as air and at the same time crisp and melt-in-the-mouth. Store in an airtight container.

For a finer texture, replace the granulated sugar with superfine sugar.

MAKES 13

4 egg whites

pinch of salt

generous 1/2 cup granulated sugar

generous 1/2 cup superfine sugar

1 1/4 cups heavy cream,
  lightly whipped

Preheat the oven to 250°F/120°C. Line 3 cookie sheets with nonstick parchment paper.

Using a hand-held electric whisk or balloon whisk, beat the egg whites and salt together in a large, clean bowl until stiff—you should be able to turn the bowl upside down without the egg whites moving.

Whisk in the granulated sugar, a little at a time—the meringue should start to look glossy at this stage.

Sprinkle in the superfine sugar, a little at a time, and continue whisking until all the sugar has been incorporated and the meringue is thick, white, and stands in tall peaks.

Transfer the meringue mixture to a pastry bag fitted with a 3/4-inch/2-cm star tip. Pipe 26 small whirls onto the prepared cookie sheets.

Bake in the preheated oven for 1 1/2 hours, or until the meringues are pale golden in color and can be easily lifted off the paper. Turn off the oven and leave the meringues inside overnight.

Just before serving, sandwich the meringues together in pairs with the whipped cream and arrange on a serving plate.

PEACH AND PECAN PASTRIES

MAKES 8

12 oz/350 g ready-made puff pastry,
   thawed if frozen

all-purpose flour, for dusting

3 fresh ripe peaches

2/3 cup sour cream

oil for greasing

4 tbsp light brown sugar

4 tbsp pecan halves, toasted and
   finely chopped

beaten egg, for sealing and glazing

superfine sugar, for sprinkling

These sweet empanadas have a
creamy, fruity filling and a hint of
crunchy nut. You could use
apricots or mangoes in place of the
peaches, adding some extra slices of
fruit to decorate. Serve as a snack
or a dessert.

Preheat the oven to 400°F/200°C. Roll out the pastry on a lightly floured counter. Using a 6-inch/15-cm saucer as a guide, cut out 8 circles.

Cut a small cross in the stem end of each peach. Lower into a pan of boiling water and let stand for 30 seconds. Drain and cool under cold running water. Using a small, sharp knife, peel, then halve the peaches. Remove the pits and slice the flesh.

Put a spoonful of sour cream in the center of a pastry circle and top with a few peach slices. Sprinkle over a little brown sugar and some nuts. Brush each edge with a little beaten egg, fold the pastry over the filling and press the edges together to seal. Crimp the edges with the tines of a fork and prick the tops. Oil the cookie sheet.

Transfer to a cookie sheet, brush with beaten egg, and sprinkle with superfine sugar. Bake in the preheated oven for 20 minutes, or until golden brown. Serve warm.

LATTICE CAKES

Preheat the oven to 425ºF/220ºC. Grease a cookie sheet.

Roll out the pastry thinly on a lightly floured counter. Using a 3¹/₂-inch/9-cm plain pastry cutter, cut out 10–12 circles.

Cream the butter and brown sugar together in a bowl until pale and fluffy, then beat in the currants, candied peel, and allspice, if using.

Put a teaspoon of the filling in the center of each pastry circle. Draw the edge of each circle together and pinch over the filling. Reshape each cake into a circle.

Turn the cakes over and lightly roll them with the rolling pin until the currants just show through. Score with a knife into a lattice pattern.

Transfer the cakes to the prepared cookie sheet and let rest for 10–15 minutes.

Brush the cakes with the egg white, sprinkle with the superfine sugar, and bake at the top of the preheated oven for 15 minutes, or until golden brown and crisp.

Transfer to a cooling rack and sprinkle with a little more sugar, if you like. Serve immediately or let cool completely and store in an airtight container for up to 1 week. The cakes can be reheated before serving.

MAKES 10-12

14 oz/400 g ready-made puff pastry, thawed if frozen

all-purpose flour, for dusting

4 tbsp butter, softened, plus extra for greasing

generous ¹/₄ cup packed brown sugar

scant ⁵/₈ cup currants

generous ¹/₈ cup candied peel, chopped

¹/₂ tsp ground allspice (optional)

1 egg white, lightly beaten

1 tsp superfine sugar, plus extra for sprinkling (optional)

These cakes originated from cooks using up leftover foods, which were enveloped in pastry so they could be baked or fried. The filling can be any leftover fruit mixed with butter, brown sugar, and spice.

CHERRY AND GOLDEN RAISIN ROCKIES

Rock buns are always popular and they are very quick and easy to make. To be at their best, they should be eaten the day they are made.

MAKES 10

6 tbsp butter, diced and chilled, plus
    extra for greasing

scant 2 cups self-rising flour

1 tsp ground allspice

generous $3/8$ cup golden superfine
    sugar

2 oz/55 g candied cherries, quartered

$1/3$ cup golden raisins

1 egg

2 tbsp milk

raw brown sugar, for sprinkling

Preheat the oven to 400°F/200°C. Lightly grease a cookie sheet. Sift the flour and allspice together into a bowl. Rub in the butter with your fingertips until the mixture resembles fine bread crumbs. Stir in the superfine sugar, cherries, and golden raisins.

Break the egg into a bowl and whisk in the milk. Pour most of the egg mixture into the dry ingredients and mix with a fork to form a stiff, coarse dough, adding the remainder of the egg mixture if necessary.

Using 2 forks, pile the dough into 10 rocky heaps on the prepared cookie sheet. Sprinkle with raw brown sugar.

Bake in the preheated oven for 10–15 minutes, or until golden and firm to the touch. Let cool on the cookie sheet for 2 minutes, then transfer to a cooling rack and let cool completely.

PAPER-THIN FRUIT PIES

Preheat the oven to 400°F/200°C. Put the butter in a small pan over low heat and heat until just melted. Brush 4 holes of a nonstick muffin pan, 4 inches/10 cm in diameter, with a little of the melted butter.

Core and thinly slice the apple and pear, then immediately toss them in the lemon juice to prevent them turning brown.

Cut each sheet of pastry into 4 and cover with a clean, damp dish towel. Working on each pie separately, brush 4 small sheets of pastry with the melted butter. Press a pastry sheet into the base of one prepared hole of the muffin tin. Arrange the other pastry sheets on top at slightly different angles. Repeat with the remaining pastry to make another 3 pies.

Arrange the apple and pear slices alternately in the center of each pie shell and lightly crimp the edge of the pastry of each pie.

Stir the jelly and orange juice together in a small bowl until smooth, then brush over the fruit. Bake in the preheated oven for 12–15 minutes. Sprinkle with the pistachios, dust lightly with confectioners' sugar, and serve hot from the oven with light cream.

MAKES 4

4 tbsp butter or margarine

1 eating apple

1 ripe pear

2 tbsp lemon juice

4 sheets phyllo pastry, thawed
   if frozen

2 tbsp apricot jelly

1 tbsp orange juice

1 tbsp finely chopped pistachios

2 tsp confectioners' sugar, for dusting

light cream, to serve

These extra-crisp phyllo pastry shells, filled with slices of fresh fruit and glazed with apricot jelly, are a delicious treat.

BANANA CREAM PROFITEROLES

SERVES 4

DOUGH

5 tbsp butter, diced, plus extra
   for greasing

2/3 cup water, plus extra
   for sprinkling

1/2 cup white bread flour, sifted

2 eggs

CHOCOLATE SAUCE

3¹/2 oz/100 g semisweet chocolate,
   broken into pieces

2 tbsp water

4 tbsp confectioners' sugar

2 tbsp butter

FILLING

1¹/4 cups heavy cream

1 banana, peeled

2 tbsp confectioners' sugar

2 tbsp crème de banane

Preheat the oven to 425°F/220°C. Lightly grease a cookie sheet and sprinkle with a little water.

To make the dough, put the water and butter in a pan over low heat and heat until the butter has melted. Bring to a rolling boil. Remove from the heat and add the flour, all at once, beating well until the mixture leaves the side of the pan and forms a ball. Let cool slightly. Gradually beat in the eggs until the dough is smooth and glossy.

Spoon the paste into a large pastry bag fitted with a ¹/2-inch/1-cm plain tip.

Pipe about 18 small balls of the paste onto the prepared cookie sheet, spaced well apart to allow for spreading. Bake in the preheated oven for 15-20 minutes until crisp and golden. Make a small slit in each one for the steam to escape, then transfer to a cooling rack and let cool.

Meanwhile, to make the sauce, put all the sauce ingredients in a heatproof bowl set over a pan of barely simmering water and heat, stirring constantly, until combined and smooth.

To make the filling, whip the cream in a bowl until soft peaks form. Mash the banana with the confectioners' sugar and liqueur in a separate bowl. Fold into the cream. Transfer the filling to a pastry bag fitted with a ¹/2-inch/1-cm plain tip. Pipe the filling into the profiteroles. Serve with the hot sauce poured over.

Chocolate profiteroles are a popular choice. In this recipe, they are filled with a delicious banana-flavored cream—the perfect combination!

CHOCOLATE BUTTERFLY CAKES

Filled with a tangy lemon buttercream, these appealing little cakes will become an all-time favorite with both adults and children.

For a chocolate buttercream, beat the butter and confectioners' sugar together, then beat in 1 oz/25 g melted semisweet chocolate.

MAKES 12

8 tbsp soft margarine

1/2 cup superfine sugar

scant 1 5/8 cups self-rising flour

2 large eggs

2 tbsp unsweetened cocoa

1 oz/25 g semisweet chocolate, melted

confectioners' sugar, for dusting

LEMON BUTTERCREAM

6 tbsp butter, preferably unsalted, softened

1 3/8 cups confectioners' sugar, sifted

grated rind of 1/2 lemon

1 tbsp lemon juice

Preheat the oven to 350°F/180°C. Line a shallow 12-hole muffin pan with muffin paper cases.

Put all the cake ingredients, except the melted chocolate and confectioners' sugar, in a large bowl. Using a hand-held electric whisk, beat until the batter is just smooth. Beat in the melted chocolate.

Divide the batter equally between the paper cases, filling each three-quarters full. Bake in the preheated oven for 15 minutes, or until springy to the touch. Transfer to a cooling rack and let cool.

Meanwhile, to make the lemon buttercream, beat the butter in a bowl until pale and fluffy, then gradually beat in the confectioners' sugar. Beat in the lemon rind, then gradually add the lemon juice, beating well.

When cool, using a serrated knife, cut the top off each cake. Cut each cake top in half. Spread or pipe the buttercream over the cut surface of each cake and push the 2 cut pieces of cake top into the frosting to form wings. Dust with confectioners' sugar.

CHOCOLATE HAZELNUT PALMIERS

MAKES 26

butter, for greasing

13 oz/375 g ready-made puff pastry,
   thawed if frozen

all-purpose flour, for dusting

8 tbsp chocolate hazelnut spread

1/2 cup chopped toasted hazelnuts

2 tbsp superfine sugar

These delicious chocolate and
hazelnut cookies are very simple to
make, yet so effective. For very young
children, leave out the chopped nuts.

Preheat the oven to 425°F/220°C. Grease a cookie sheet. Roll out the pastry on a lightly floured counter into a rectangle about 15 x 9 inches/38 x 23 cm.

Spread the chocolate hazelnut spread over the pastry using a palette knife, then sprinkle the hazelnuts over the top.

Roll up one long side of the pastry to the center, then the other, so that they meet in the center. Where the pieces meet, dampen the edges with a little water to join them. Using a sharp knife, cut into 26 thin slices. Transfer each slice to the prepared cookie sheet and flatten slightly with a palette knife. Sprinkle with the sugar.

Bake in the preheated oven for 10-15 minutes, or until golden. Transfer to a cooling rack and let cool.

MOCHA **ROLLS**

Preheat the oven to 350°F/180°C. For the sponge cake, base-line a 12 x 8 x 1½-inch/30 x 20 x 4-cm rectangular cake pan with nonstick parchment paper. Put the eggs, egg white, and sugar in a heatproof bowl, set over a pan of barely simmering water and whisk until thick and pale. Remove from the heat, then whisk until cool. Sift over the flour and fold in. Fold in the melted butter, a little at a time.

Pour the batter into the prepared pan and bake in the preheated oven for 25–30 minutes until the cake is springy to the touch and has shrunk slightly from the sides of the pan. Remove from the oven and transfer to a cooling rack, still standing on the lining paper, to cool.

Meanwhile, put 2 tablespoons of the coffee into a small heatproof bowl and sprinkle the gelatin on the surface. Let soften for 2 minutes, then set the bowl over a pan of barely simmering water and stir until the gelatin has dissolved. Remove from the heat. Put the remaining coffee, liqueur, and ricotta cheese in a food processor or blender and process until smooth. Add the gelatin mixture in a continuous stream and process briefly. Scrape the mixture into a bowl, cover with plastic wrap, and let chill for 1–1½ hours until set.

Peel the lining paper off the cake. Using a knife, cut the cake in half horizontally. Trim off any dried edges. Cut each piece of cake in half lengthwise. Put each piece between 2 sheets of parchment paper and roll with a rolling pin to make it more flexible. Spread one side of each cake piece with a ¼-inch/5-mm thick layer of the coffee filling, leaving a ¼-inch/5-mm margin all around. Cut each strip across into 4 pieces, to give a total of 16. Roll up each piece from the short end.

Put one roll seam-side down on a metal palette knife and hold it over the bowl of melted white chocolate. Spoon the chocolate over the roll to coat. Transfer to a sheet of parchment paper. Repeat with the remaining rolls.

Spoon the semisweet chocolate into a waxed paper pastry bag fitted with a small, plain tip and pipe zig-zags along the rolls. Let set.

MAKES 16

²/₃ cup cold strong black coffee

1 tbsp gelatin

1 tsp Kahlúa or other coffee-flavored liqueur

1 cup ricotta cheese

10 oz/280 g white chocolate, melted

1 oz/25 g semisweet chocolate, melted

SPONGE CAKE

3 eggs, plus 1 egg white

generous ³/₈ cup superfine sugar

scant ³/₄ cup all-purpose flour

2 tbsp butter, melted

Semisweet and white chocolate are combined with coffee and Kahlúa in these attractive sponge-cake rolls.

RASPBERRY CHOCOLATE ECLAIRS

These small éclairs are perfect for serving at a summer tea party. They look particularly appealing arranged on a pretty serving plate.

MAKES 20-24

2/3 cup water

4 tbsp butter

1/2 cup all-purpose flour, sifted

2 eggs, beaten

FILLING AND TOPPING

3/4 cup heavy cream

1 tbsp confectioners' sugar

6 oz/175 g fresh raspberries

3 oz/85 g semisweet chocolate,
   melted

Preheat the oven to 425°F/220°C. Sprinkle 2 cookie sheets with a little water. Put the water and butter in a pan over low heat and heat until the butter has melted. Bring to a rolling boil. Remove from the heat and add the flour, all at once, beating well until the mixture leaves the side of the pan and forms a ball. Let cool slightly. Gradually beat in the eggs until the dough is smooth and glossy.

Spoon into a pastry bag fitted with a 1/2-inch/1-cm plain tip. Pipe 20-24 x 3-inch/7.5-cm lengths onto the prepared cookie sheets, spaced well apart to allow for spreading. Bake in the preheated oven for 10 minutes. Reduce the temperature to 375°F/190°C and bake for an additional 20 minutes, or until crisp and golden. Split each éclair for the steam to escape, then transfer to a cooling rack and let cool.

To make the filling, whip the cream and sugar together in a bowl until thick. Spoon into the éclairs. Put a few raspberries in each éclair. Spread a little melted chocolate on each éclair and let set before serving.

COCONUT AND CHERRY CAKES

Preheat the oven to 350°F/180°C. Line 1 or 2 muffin pans with 8 muffin paper cases. Cream the butter and sugar together in a bowl until pale and fluffy, then stir in the milk.

Gradually beat in the eggs. Sift in the flour and baking powder and fold in with the coconut. Gently fold in most of the cherries. Spoon the batter into the paper cases and sprinkle the remaining cherries on top.

Bake in the preheated oven for 20-25 minutes, or until well risen, golden, and springy to the touch. Transfer to a cooling rack and let cool.

MAKES 8

8 tbsp butter, softened

generous $1/2$ cup golden superfine
   sugar

2 tbsp milk

2 eggs, beaten

scant $5/8$ cup self-rising flour

$1/2$ tsp baking powder

$2/3$ cup dry unsweetened coconut

4 oz/115 g candied cherries, quartered

Coconut and candied cherries make
these little cakes really moist, and give
them a sweet flavor that will make
them a hit with children.

family cakes

Everyone has his or her favorite family cake. It can be the cake that evokes memories of munching happily in a cosy kitchen surrounded by the sweet aroma of baking, or simply the cake that can be depended on time and time again to cheer up your day with the first mouthful. From the classic Sponge Cake to Moist Chocolate Cake, this chapter contains a collection of cakes that provide the perfect starting point for beginners.

SPONGE CAKE

Preheat the oven to 350°F/180°C. Grease 2 x 8-inch/20-cm round shallow cake pans and base-line with waxed or nonstick parchment paper.

Cream the butter and sugar together in a bowl until pale and fluffy. Add the eggs, a little at a time, beating well after each addition.

Sift the flour and salt together, then gently fold into the mixture using a metal spoon or a spatula. Divide the batter between the prepared pans and smooth the surfaces.

Bake both cakes on the same shelf in the center of the preheated oven for 25–30 minutes until well risen, golden brown, and beginning to shrink from the side of each pan.

Let stand in the pans for 1 minute. Using a palette knife, loosen the cakes from around the edge of each pan. Turn out the cakes onto a clean dish towel, remove the lining paper and invert onto a cooling rack (this prevents the cooling rack from marking the top of the cakes).

When completely cool, sandwich together with the jelly and sprinkle with the sugar. The cake is delicious when freshly baked, but any remaining cake can be stored in an airtight tin for up to 1 week.

MAKES 8-10 SLICES

3/4 cup butter, at room temperature, plus extra for greasing

scant 1 cup superfine sugar

3 eggs, beaten

scant 1 1/4 cups self-rising flour

pinch of salt

TO SERVE

3 tbsp raspberry jelly

1 tbsp superfine or confectioners' sugar

This cake is traditionally made by the creaming method, although you can easily make it by the all-in-one method –just make sure that the butter is softened, add 1 teaspoon of baking powder to the flour and then beat all the ingredients together with an electric mixer. It makes a useful base for a child's birthday cake.

UPSIDE-DOWN DESSERT

Preheat the oven to 350°F/180°C. Grease a 10-inch/25-cm round cake pan and base-line with nonstick parchment paper.

Cream 4 tbsp of the butter and the brown sugar together in a bowl until pale and fluffy. Spread over the base of the prepared pan. Put a hazelnut in each apricot half and invert onto the base. The apricots should cover the whole surface.

Cream the remaining butter and the raw brown sugar in a bowl until pale and fluffy. Add the eggs, a little at a time, beating well after each addition. Sift the flour, then gently fold into the mixture with the hazelnuts and milk using a metal spoon or a spatula. Spread the batter over the apricots.

Bake in the center of the preheated oven for 45 minutes, or until golden brown and well risen. Run a knife round the edge of the pudding and invert onto a warmed plate. Serve warm with custard or cream.

SERVES 6-8

1 cup unsalted butter, plus extra for
   greasing

generous 1/4 cup packed brown sugar

14-16 hazelnuts

1 lb 5 oz/600 g canned apricot halves,
   drained

scant 1 cup raw brown sugar

3 eggs, beaten

scant 1 1/4 cups self-rising flour

generous 1/2 cup ground hazelnuts

2 tbsp milk

custard or heavy cream, to serve

Sometimes known as an "upside-down cake," this is a creamed cake batter that is baked with fruit under it, so that when it is turned out, the fruit is on top and looks decorative. It has a lovely rich butter and sugar topping as well, which gives the pudding an attractive, glossy appearance. You could use pear halves with walnuts instead of apricots and hazelnuts.

BANANA AND CRANBERRY LOAF

Preheat the oven to 350°F/180°C. Grease a 2-lb/900-g loaf pan and base-line with nonstick parchment paper.

Sift the flour and baking powder together into a bowl. Stir in the brown sugar, bananas, candied peel, nuts, and dried cranberries.

Stir the orange juice, eggs, and oil together in a separate bowl until well combined. Add the mixture to the dry ingredients and mix until thoroughly blended. Spoon the mixture into the prepared loaf pan and smooth the surface.

Bake in the preheated oven for 1 hour, or until firm to the touch or a skewer inserted into the center of the loaf comes out clean.

Turn out the loaf onto a cooling rack and let cool.

Mix the confectioners' sugar with a little water in a small bowl and drizzle the frosting over the loaf. Sprinkle the orange rind over the top. Let the frosting set before slicing and serving.

SERVES 8

butter, for greasing

scant 1⁵/₈ cups self-rising flour

¹/₂ tsp baking powder

scant ²/₃ cup packed brown sugar

2 bananas, peeled and mashed

generous ¹/₄ cup candied peel

generous ¹/₄ cup chopped mixed nuts

generous ³/₈ cup dried cranberries

5–6 tbsp orange juice

2 eggs, beaten

²/₃ cup sunflower-seed oil

³/₄ cup confectioners' sugar, sifted

grated rind of 1 orange

The addition of chopped nuts, candied peel, fresh orange juice, and dried cranberries makes this a rich, moist bread.

This bread will keep for a couple of days. Wrap it carefully and store in a cool, dry place.

RASPBERRY **DESSERT** CAKE

SERVES 9–10

generous 1 cup bittersweet chocolate,
   broken into pieces

1 cup unsalted butter, plus extra
   for oiling

1 tbsp strong, dark coffee

5 eggs

generous 1/2 cup golden superfine
   sugar

scant 2/3 cup all-purpose flour

1 tsp ground cinnamon

1 cup fresh raspberries, plus extra to
   serve

confectioners' sugar, for dusting

whipped cream, to serve

Preheat the oven to 325ºF/160ºC. Grease a 9-inch/23-cm cake tin and line the base with non-stick baking paper. Put the chocolate, butter, and coffee in a small, heatproof bowl, set the bowl over a pan of barely simmering water and heat until melted. Remove from the heat, stir, and leave to cool slightly.

Beat the eggs and superfine sugar together in a separate bowl until pale and thick. Gently fold in the chocolate mixture.

Sift the flour and cinnamon into another bowl, then fold into the chocolate mixture. Pour into the prepared tin and sprinkle the raspberries evenly over the top.

Bake in the preheated oven for about 35-45 minutes, or until the cake is well risen and springy to the touch. Leave to cool in the tin for 15 minutes before turning out onto a large serving plate. Dust with confectioners' sugar before serving with extra fresh raspberries and whipped cream.

If fresh raspberries are not available, frozen raspberries may be used. Since these will be softer than fresh fruit, take care to thaw them thoroughly and drain off any excess juice.

CHOCOLATE CHIP BROWNIES

Choose a good-quality semisweet chocolate for these chocolate chip brownies to give them a rich flavor that is not too sweet. The brownie won't be completely firm in the center when it is removed from the oven, but it will set when it has cooled.

MAKES 12

1 cup butter, softened, plus
  extra for greasing

5¹/₂ oz/150 g semisweet chocolate,
  broken into pieces

2 cups all-purpose flour

¹/₂ cup superfine sugar

4 eggs, beaten

¹/₂ cup chopped pistachios

3¹/₂ oz/100 g white chocolate,
  coarsely chopped

confectioners' sugar, for dusting

Preheat the oven to 350°F/180°C. Lightly grease a 9-inch/23-cm square baking pan and line with waxed paper.

Melt the semisweet chocolate and butter in a heatproof bowl set over a pan of barely simmering water. Let cool slightly.

Sift the flour into a separate bowl and stir in the superfine sugar.

Stir the eggs into the melted chocolate mixture, then pour this mixture into the flour mixture, beating well. Stir in the pistachios and white chocolate, then pour the batter into the pan, spreading it evenly into the corners.

Bake in the preheated oven for 30–35 minutes until firm to the touch. Let cool in the pan for 20 minutes, then turn out onto a cooling rack.

Let cool completely, then cut into 12 pieces and dust with confectioners' sugar.

STRAWBERRY ROLL

SERVES 8

3 large eggs

generous $^1/_2$ cup superfine sugar

scant 1 cup all-purpose flour

1 tbsp hot water

FILLING

$^3/_4$ cup mascarpone cheese

1 tsp almond extract

8 oz/225 g small strawberries

TO DECORATE

1 tbsp slivered almonds, toasted

1 tsp confectioners' sugar

Serve this moist, light sponge cake rolled up with a creamy almond and strawberry filling for a delicious tea-time treat.

Preheat the oven to 425°F/ 220°C. Line a 14-x-10-inch/35-x-25-cm jelly roll pan with nonstick parchment paper.

Put the eggs and superfine sugar in a heatproof bowl set over a pan of barely simmering water. Using a hand-held electric whisk, beat together until thick and pale—the mixture should leave a trail when the whisk is lifted.

Remove the bowl from the pan. Sift in the flour and fold into the egg mixture with the hot water. Pour the batter into the prepared pan and bake in the preheated oven for 8-10 minutes until golden and set.

Turn out the cake onto a sheet of nonstick parchment paper. Peel off the lining paper and roll up the sponge cake tightly, encasing the parchment paper. Wrap in a clean dish towel and let cool.

Mix the mascarpone and almond extract together. Reserving a few strawberries for decoration, wash, hull, and slice the remainder. Chill with the mascarpone mixture in the refrigerator until required.

Unroll the cake, spread with the mascarpone mixture and sprinkle with sliced strawberries. Roll the cake up again and transfer to a serving plate. Sprinkle with the almonds and dust with confectioners' sugar. Decorate with the reserved strawberries.

CLEMENTINE CAKE

Preheat the oven to 350°F/ 180°C. Grease a 7-inch/18-cm round cake pan and base-line with nonstick parchment paper.

Finely chop the clementine rind. Cream the butter, sugar, and clementine rind together in a bowl until pale and fluffy.

Add the eggs, a little at a time, beating well after each addition. Gently fold in the flour, ground almonds, and cream. Spoon the batter into the prepared pan.

Bake in the preheated oven for 55-60 minutes, or until a fine skewer inserted into the center comes out clean. Let cool slightly.

Meanwhile, to make the glaze, put the clementine juice in a small pan with the superfine sugar over medium-low heat. Bring to a boil, then reduce the heat and simmer for 5 minutes.

Turn out the cake onto a cooling rack. Drizzle the glaze over the cake until it has been absorbed and sprinkle with the crushed sugar lumps. Let cool completely before serving.

SERVES 8

3/4 cup butter, softened, plus extra for greasing

rind of 2 clementines

scant 1 cup superfine sugar

3 eggs, lightly beaten

scant 1 1/4 cups self-rising flour

3 tbsp ground almonds

3 tbsp light cream

GLAZE AND TOPPING

6 tbsp clementine juice

2 tbsp superfine sugar

3 white sugar lumps, crushed

This cake is flavored with clementine rind and juice, creating a rich, buttery cake bursting with fruit flavor. Orange would also work well.

If you prefer, chop the rind from the clementines in a food processor along with the sugar. Tip the mixture into a bowl with the butter and start to cream the mixture.

CARROT CAKE

Preheat the oven to 350°F/180°C. Grease an 8-inch/20-cm square cake pan and line with nonstick parchment paper.

Sift the flour, salt, and cinnamon into a large bowl and stir in the brown sugar. Add the eggs and oil to the dry ingredients and mix well.

Stir in the carrot, coconut, and chopped walnuts.

Pour the batter into the prepared pan and bake in the preheated oven for 20–25 minutes, or until just firm to the touch. Let cool in the pan.

Meanwhile, to make the cream cheese frosting, beat the butter, cream cheese, confectioners' sugar, and lemon juice together in a bowl until light, fluffy, and creamy.

Turn out the cake from the pan. Spread the top with the frosting and decorate with a few walnut pieces. Cut into 12 bars or slices.

MAKES 12 BARS/SLICES

butter, for greasing

scant 1 cup self-rising flour

pinch of salt

1 tsp ground cinnamon

scant $2/3$ cup packed brown sugar

2 eggs

generous $1/3$ cup sunflower-seed oil

6 oz/175 g finely grated carrot

$1/4$ cup grated coconut

2 tbsp chopped walnuts

walnut pieces, to decorate

CREAM CHEESE FROSTING

4 tbsp butter, softened

$1/4$ cup cream cheese

$1^1/4$ cups confectioners' sugar, sifted

1 tsp lemon juice

This classic favorite is always popular when served for afternoon tea. It is also good served as a dessert. For a more moist cake, replace the coconut with a coarsely mashed banana.

CRUNCHY **FRUIT** CAKE

Cornmeal adds texture to this cake, flavored with dried fruit and pine nuts, as well as a golden yellow color. For a more crumbly cake, omit the cornmeal and use scant 1¼ cups self-rising flour instead.

SERVES 8

9 tbsp butter, softened, plus extra for
   greasing

generous ½ cup superfine sugar

2 eggs, beaten

generous ³/₈ cup self-rising flour, sifted

1 tsp baking powder

½ cup cornmeal

9 oz/250 g mixed dried fruit

generous ⅛ cup pine nuts

grated rind of 1 lemon

4 tbsp lemon juice

2 tbsp milk

Preheat the oven to 350°F/180°C. Grease a 7-inch/18-cm round cake pan and base-line with nonstick parchment paper.

Cream the butter and sugar together in a bowl until pale and fluffy. Add the eggs, a little at a time, beating well after each addition.

Gently fold the flour, baking powder, and cornmeal into the mixture until well combined.

Gently stir in the dried fruit, pine nuts, grated lemon rind, lemon juice, and milk.

Spoon the batter into the prepared pan and smooth the surface with a knife.

Bake in the preheated oven for 1 hour, or until a skewer inserted into the center of the cake comes out clean.

Let the cake cool in the pan before turning out and serving.

LEMON **SYRUP** CAKE

Preheat the oven to 350°F/180°C. Grease an 8-inch/20-cm round loose-bottom cake pan and base-line with nonstick parchment paper.

Sift the flour and baking powder together into a bowl and stir in the superfine sugar.

Beat the eggs, sour cream, lemon rind and juice, and oil together in a separate bowl. Pour the egg mixture into the dry ingredients and mix well until evenly combined.

Pour the batter into the prepared pan and bake in the preheated oven for 45-60 minutes until risen and golden brown.

Meanwhile, to make the syrup, combine the confectioners' sugar and lemon juice in a small pan. Stir over low heat until just starting to bubble and turn syrupy.

As soon as the cake comes out of the oven, prick the surface with a fine skewer, then brush the syrup over the top. Let the cake cool completely in the pan before turning out and serving.

SERVES 6-8

butter, for greasing

scant 1⁵/₈ cups all-purpose flour

2 tsp baking powder

generous 1¹/₈ cups superfine sugar

4 eggs

²/₃ cup sour cream

grated rind of 1 large lemon

4 tbsp lemon juice

²/₃ cup sunflower-seed oil

SYRUP

4 tbsp confectioners' sugar

3 tbsp lemon juice

The lovely light and tangy flavor of the sponge cake is balanced by the lemony syrup poured over the top.

Pricking the surface of the hot cake with a skewer ensures that the syrup seeps right into the cake and the full flavor is absorbed.

MOIST CHOCOLATE CAKE

Preheat the oven to 325°F/160°C. Grease a 3$^{1}/_{2}$-cup ovenproof bowl. Cream the butter, sugar, and vanilla extract together in a bowl until pale and fluffy. Add the eggs, a little at a time, beating well after each addition.

Melt the semisweet chocolate in a heatproof bowl set over a pan of barely simmering water. Gradually stir in the buttermilk until well combined. Remove from the heat and let cool slightly.

Sift the flour, baking soda, and salt together into a separate bowl. Using a metal spoon or spatula, gently fold in the chocolate mixture alternately with the flour mixture into the creamed mixture, a little at a time. Spoon the cake batter into the prepared ovenproof bowl and smooth the surface.

Bake in the preheated oven for 50 minutes, or until a skewer inserted into the center of the cake comes out clean. Turn out onto a cooling rack and let cool.

Meanwhile, to make the frosting, put the marshmallows and milk in a small pan over very low heat and heat until the marshmallows have melted. Remove from the heat and let cool.

Whisk the egg whites in a large, clean bowl until soft peaks form, then add the sugar and continue whisking until stiff peaks form. Fold the egg white mixture into the cooled marshmallow mixture and set aside for 10 minutes.

When the cake is cool, cover the top and side with the marshmallow frosting. Top with grated milk chocolate.

MAKES ONE 6-INCH/ 15-CM CAKE

6$^{1}/_{2}$ tbsp butter, preferably unsalted, plus extra for greasing

generous 1$^{1}/_{8}$ cups superfine sugar

$^{1}/_{2}$ tsp vanilla extract

2 eggs, lightly beaten

3 oz/85 g semisweet chocolate, broken into pieces

5 tbsp buttermilk

scant 1$^{1}/_{4}$ cups self-rising flour

$^{1}/_{2}$ tsp baking soda

pinch of salt

2 oz/55 g milk chocolate, grated, to decorate

MARSHMALLOW FROSTING

6 oz/175 g white marshmallows

1 tbsp milk

2 egg whites

2 tbsp superfine sugar

The sweetness of the whipped marshmallow frosting complements the mouthwatering flavor of this moist plain chocolate sponge.

GINGERBREAD

This spicy gingerbread is made even more moist and flavorful by the addition of chopped fresh apples. Serve as a midafternoon snack. If you enjoy the flavor of ginger, try adding 1 tablespoon finely chopped preserved ginger to the mixture.

MAKES 12 BARS

3/4 cup butter, plus extra
   for greasing
scant 1 cup packed light brown sugar
2 tbsp molasses
scant 1^5/8 cups all-purpose flour
1 tsp baking powder
2 tsp baking soda
2 tsp ground ginger
2/3 cup milk
1 egg, lightly beaten
2 eating apples, peeled, chopped, and
   tossed in 1 tbsp lemon juice

Preheat the oven to 325°F/160°C. Grease a 9-inch/23-cm square cake pan and line with nonstick parchment paper.

Heat the butter, sugar, and molasses in a pan over low heat, stirring, until melted. Remove from the heat and let cool.

Sift the flour, baking powder, baking soda, and ginger together into a large bowl.

Stir in the milk, egg, and the butter mixture, followed by the apples tossed in the lemon juice.

Mix together gently, then pour the mixture into the prepared pan.

Bake in the preheated oven for 30–35 minutes until well risen and a skewer inserted into the center of the cake comes out clean.

Let the cake cool in the pan before turning out and cutting into 12 bars.

YOGURT CAKE

Preheat the oven to 350°F/180°C. Oil an 8-inch/20-cm round loose-bottom cake pan and line with waxed paper.

Put the yogurt, oil, superfine sugar, flour, eggs, and lemon rind in a large bowl or food processor and beat together or process until smooth.

Turn the batter into the prepared cake pan and bake in the preheated oven for 1¼ hours, or until golden brown and a skewer inserted into the center of the cake comes out clean.

Meanwhile, put the lemon juice and granulated sugar in a pan over low heat and heat until the sugar has dissolved. Bring to a boil, then reduce the heat and simmer for 2–3 minutes. Stir in the honey.

When the cake is cooked, carefully turn out and transfer to a cooling rack set over a tray. Prick the top of the cake all over with a fine skewer. If necessary, reheat the lemon syrup, then pour the hot syrup over the warm cake and let cool. Sprinkle over the slivered almonds to decorate before serving. Serve with strained plain yogurt.

SERVES 8

⅔ cup sunflower-seed or corn oil, plus extra for oiling

⅔ cup strained plain yogurt, plus extra to serve

generous 1¼ cups superfine sugar

scant 2 cups self-rising flour

2 eggs

LEMON SYRUP

juice and finely grated rind of 2 large lemons

generous ⅓ cup granulated sugar

2 tbsp honey

¼ cup toasted slivered almonds, to decorate

This is a light, moist cake, finished with a tangy lemon and honey syrup.

WALNUT CAKE

SERVES 12

8 tbsp butter, softened, plus extra for
   greasing

scant 1 cup self-rising flour

$^1/_2$ tsp ground cinnamon

$^1/_4$ tsp ground cloves

generous $^1/_2$ cup superfine sugar

4 eggs

2 cups walnut pieces,
   finely chopped

ORANGE SYRUP

juice and pared rind of 1 orange

generous $^1/_2$ cup granulated sugar

2 tbsp brandy

Preheat the oven to 375°F/190°C. Grease and base-line a deep roasting pan measuring 10 x 7 inches/25 x 18 cm with waxed paper.

Sift the flour, cinnamon, and cloves together into a bowl. Cream the butter and superfine sugar together in a large bowl until pale and fluffy. Add the eggs, one at a time, beating well after each addition. Using a metal spoon or spatula, gently fold in the flour mixture, then fold in the chopped walnuts.

Turn the batter into the prepared pan and bake in the preheated oven for 30 minutes, or until risen and springy to the touch.

Meanwhile, to make the orange syrup, put the orange juice in a measuring cup and make up to $^2/_3$ cup with water. Pour into a pan, add the granulated sugar and the pared orange rind and heat over low heat until the sugar has dissolved. Bring to a boil and boil for 6 minutes until the mixture begins to thicken. Remove from the heat and stir in the brandy.

When the cake is cooked, prick the surface all over with a fine skewer, then strain the hot syrup over the top of the cake. Leave in the pan for at least 4 hours before serving.

This moist walnut cake is made a little more special by being topped with a
fragrant orange- and brandy-flavored syrup.

STRAWBERRY CHEESECAKE

Sweet strawberries are teamed with creamy mascarpone cheese and luxurious white chocolate to make this mouthwatering cheesecake.

SERVES 8

BASE

4 tbsp butter, preferably unsalted

7 oz/200 g crushed graham crackers

1/2 cup chopped walnuts

FILLING

1 lb/450 g mascarpone cheese

2 eggs, beaten

3 tbsp superfine sugar

9 oz/250 g white chocolate, broken into pieces

10 1/2 oz/300 g strawberries, hulled and quartered

TOPPING

6 oz/175 g mascarpone cheese

ready-made chocolate caraque

16 whole strawberries

Preheat the oven to 300°F/150°C. Melt the butter in a pan over low heat and stir in the crushed cookies and nuts. Spoon into a 9-inch/23-cm round springform cake pan and press evenly over the base with the back of a spoon. Set aside.

To make the filling, beat the mascarpone cheese in a bowl until smooth, then beat in the eggs and sugar. Melt the white chocolate in a heatproof bowl set over a pan of barely simmering water, stirring until smooth. Remove from the heat and let cool slightly, then stir into the cheese mixture. Stir in the strawberries.

Spoon the mixture into the cake pan, spread out evenly and smooth the surface. Bake in the preheated oven for 1 hour, or until the filling is just firm. Turn off the oven and let the cheesecake cool inside with the door slightly ajar until completely cold.

Transfer to a serving plate and spread the mascarpone cheese on top. Decorate with chocolate caraque and the whole strawberries.

RICOTTA **CHEESECAKE**

SERVES 6-8

PIE DOUGH

8 tbsp unsalted butter, diced
   and chilled, plus extra for greasing

scant 1¹/₄ cups all-purpose flour, plus
   extra for dusting

3 tbsp superfine sugar

pinch of salt

1 egg yolk

FILLING

1 lb/450 g ricotta cheese

¹/₂ cup heavy cream

2 eggs, plus 1 egg yolk

generous ³/₈ cup superfine sugar

finely grated rind of 1 lemon

finely grated rind of 1 orange

Grease an 8-inch/20-cm round loose-bottom tart pan. To make the pie dough, sift the flour, sugar, and salt together onto a counter and make a well in the center. Add the butter and egg yolk to the well and, using your fingertips, gradually work in the flour mixture until well combined.

Gather up the dough and knead very lightly on a lightly floured counter. Cut off about one-quarter, wrap in plastic wrap, and let chill in the refrigerator. Press the remaining dough into the base of the tart pan. Chill in the refrigerator for 30 minutes.

To make the filling, beat the ricotta cheese, cream, eggs and egg yolk, sugar, and lemon and orange rinds together in a bowl. Cover with plastic wrap and chill in the refrigerator until required.

When ready to bake, preheat the oven to 375°F/190°C. Prick the base of the pastry shell all over with a fork. Line with foil, fill with baking beans, and bake in a preheated oven for 15 minutes.

Remove the the foil and beans, transfer the pan to a cooling rack and let cool.

Spoon the ricotta mixture into the pastry shell and smooth the surface. Roll out the reserved dough on a lightly floured counter and cut into strips. Arrange the strips over the filling in a lattice pattern, brushing the overlapping ends with a little water so that they stick.

Bake in the oven for 30–35 minutes until the top of the cheesecake is golden and the filling has set. Transfer to a cooling rack and let cool before carefully removing from the pan. Cut into wedges to serve.

HOT **CHOCOLATE** CHEESECAKE

Grease an 8-inch/20-cm round loose-bottom cake pan. To make the pie dough, sift the flour and cocoa together into a bowl and rub in the butter with your fingertips until the mixture resembles fine bread crumbs. Stir in the sugar and ground almonds.

Add the egg yolk and sufficient water to form a soft dough.

Roll out the dough on a lightly floured counter and use to line the prepared pan. Let chill in the refrigerator for 30 minutes.

When ready to bake, preheat the oven to 325°F/160°C. To make the filling, beat the egg yolks and sugar together in a large bowl until thick and pale. Beat in the cream cheese, ground almonds, cream, cocoa, and vanilla extract until well combined.

Whisk the egg whites in a separate large, clean bowl until stiff but not dry. Stir a little of the egg white into the cheese mixture, then fold in the remainder. Pour into the pastry shell. Bake in the oven for 1½ hours, or until well risen and just firm to the touch. Carefully remove from the pan and dust with confectioners' sugar.

Serve the cheesecake warm.

SERVES 8-10

PIE DOUGH

4 tbsp butter, plus extra for greasing

generous 1 cup all-purpose flour, plus extra for dusting

2 tbsp unsweetened cocoa

2 tbsp golden superfine sugar

generous ¼ cup ground almonds

1 egg yolk

FILLING

2 eggs, separated

generous ⅓ cup golden superfine sugar

1½ cups cream cheese

4 tbsp ground almonds

⅔ cup heavy cream

generous ¼ cup unsweetened cocoa, sifted

1 tsp vanilla extract

confectioners' sugar, for dusting

This rich cheesecake has chocolate in the pie dough and in the filling.
Your guests are sure to come back for more!

treats FOR *special occasions*

No special occasion is quite complete without the presence of a lavish sweet treat. Desserts such as torte, vacherin, and gâteau may require a little more preparation than the average sponge, but they are the perfect ending to a lovingly prepared meal, or a decadent dinner party. The mouthwatering recipes in this chapter will challenge your baking skills, unleash your creative powers, and cause a jaw or two to drop in delight!

LEMON MERINGUE PIE

Grease a 10-inch/25-cm round fluted tart pan. Roll out the pastry on a lightly floured counter into a circle 2 inches/5 cm larger than the tart pan. Ease the pastry into the pan without stretching and press down lightly into the corners. Roll the rolling pin over the pan to neaten and trim the edge. Prick the base of the tart shell all over with a fork. Let chill in the refrigerator for 20–30 minutes.

When ready to bake, put a cookie sheet in the oven and preheat the oven to 400°F/200°C. Line the pastry shell with parchment paper and fill with baking beans. Bake on the hot cookie sheet in the preheated oven for 15 minutes. Remove the beans and paper and bake for an additional 10 minutes until the pastry is dry and just coloring. Remove from the oven and reduce the temperature to 300°F/150°C.

Put the cornstarch, superfine sugar, and lemon rind into a pan. Pour in a little of the water and blend to a smooth paste. Gradually add the remaining water and the lemon juice. Bring to a boil over medium heat, stirring constantly. Reduce the heat and simmer gently for 1 minute until smooth and glossy. Remove from the heat and beat in the egg yolks, one at a time, then beat in the butter. Put the pan in a bowl of cold water to cool the filling. When cool, spoon the mixture into the pastry shell.

To make the meringue, using a hand-held electric whisk, beat the egg whites in a large, clean bowl until thick and soft peaks form. Gradually add the superfine sugar, beating well after each addition—the mixture should be glossy and firm. Spoon the meringue over the filling to cover it completely and make a seal with the pastry shell. Swirl the meringue into peaks and sprinkle with the granulated sugar.

Bake in the preheated oven for 20–30 minutes until the meringue is crisp and pale gold (the center should still be soft). Let cool slightly before serving.

SERVES 8–10

4 tbsp unsalted butter, diced, plus
    extra for greasing

9 oz/250 g ready-rolled short-crust
    pastry, thawed if frozen

all-purpose flour, for dusting

3 tbsp cornstarch

generous $^3/_8$ cup superfine sugar

grated rind of 3 lemons

$1^1/_4$ cups cold water

$^2/_3$ cup lemon juice

3 egg yolks

MERINGUE

3 egg whites

scant 1 cup superfine sugar

1 tsp golden granulated sugar

This pie is a great favorite. As it is a complicated recipe, it is worth making a good-sized one. Try serving warm with some vanilla ice cream.

RICH **FRUIT** CAKE

Serve this moist, fruit-laden cake for a special occasion. It would also make an excellent Christmas cake.

SERVES 8-10

butter or margarine, for greasing

4¹/₂ oz/125 g pitted dates

3¹/₂ oz/100 g no-soak dried prunes

scant 1 cup unsweetened
    orange juice

2 tbsp molasses

1 tsp finely grated lemon rind

1 tsp finely grated orange rind

generous 2 cups self-rising
    whole wheat flour

1 tsp ground allspice

generous ³/₄ cup raisins

scant 1 cup golden raisins

generous ¹/₂ cup currants

scant 1 cup dried cranberries

3 large eggs, separated

TO DECORATE

1 tbsp apricot jelly, softened

confectioners' sugar, for dusting

6 oz/175 g ready-to-roll fondant
    frosting

strips of orange rind

strips of lemon rind

Preheat the oven to 325°F/160°C. Grease and line a deep 8-inch/20-cm round cake pan with waxed paper. Chop the dates and prunes and put in a pan. Pour over the orange juice and bring to a boil over medium-low heat. Reduce the heat and simmer for 10 minutes. Remove from the heat and beat the fruit mixture until puréed. Add the molasses and lemon and orange rinds. Let cool.

Sift the flour and allspice together into a bowl and add the raisins, golden raisins, currants, and cranberries. When the date and prune mixture is cool, beat in the egg yolks. Whisk the egg whites in a separate large, clean bowl until stiff peaks form. Spoon the fruit mixture into the dry ingredients and mix together. Gently fold in the egg whites.

Transfer the batter to the prepared pan and bake in the preheated oven for 1¹/₂ hours. Let cool in the pan.

Turn out the cake from the pan and brush the top with jelly. Dust the counter with confectioners' sugar and roll out the frosting thinly. Lay over the cake top and trim the edges. Decorate with orange and lemon rind.

RASPBERRY LAYER CAKE

SERVES 10

3 egg whites

scant 1 cup superfine sugar

1 tsp cornstarch

1 oz/25 g semisweet chocolate, grated

FILLING

6 oz/175 g semisweet chocolate,
  plus extra to decorate, broken
  into pieces

2 cups heavy cream, whipped

10^1/2 oz/300 g fresh raspberries

Preheat the oven to 275°F/140°C. Draw 3 rectangles, measuring 4 x 10 inches/10 x 25 cm, on sheets of nonstick parchment paper and put on 2 cookie sheets.

Whisk the egg whites in a large, clean bowl until soft peaks form, then gradually whisk in half the sugar and continue whisking until very stiff and glossy.

Gently fold in the remaining sugar, the cornstarch, and grated chocolate with a metal spoon or a palette knife.

Spoon the meringue mixture into a pastry bag fitted with a 1/2-inch/ 1-cm plain tip and pipe lines across the parchment paper rectangles.

Bake in the preheated oven for 1^1/2 hours, changing the position of the cookie sheets halfway through. Without opening the oven, turn off the oven and let the meringues cool in the inside oven, then peel off the parchment paper.

To make the filling, melt the chocolate in a heatproof bowl set over a pan of barely simmering water and spread it over 2 of the meringue layers. Let set.

Put a chocolate-coated meringue on a plate and top with about one-third of the cream and raspberries. Gently put the second chocolate-coated meringue on top and spread with half the remaining cream and raspberries. Put the remaining meringue on top and decorate with the remaining cream and raspberries.

Melt a few extra pieces of chocolate in a heatproof bowl set over a pan of barely simmering water. Drizzle over the top of the vacherin and serve.

PEACH MELBA MERINGUE ROLL

SERVES 8

sunflower-seed oil, for oiling

COULIS

12 oz/350 g fresh raspberries

1 cup confectioners' sugar

MERINGUE

2 tsp cornstarch

1 1/2 cups superfine sugar

5 large egg whites

1 tsp cider vinegar

FILLING

3 peaches, peeled, pitted,
and chopped

9 oz/250 g fresh raspberries

scant 1 cup sour cream

2/3 cup heavy cream

Preheat the oven to 300°F/150°C. Oil a 14 x 10-inch/35 x 25-cm jelly roll pan and line with nonstick parchment paper. To make the coulis, process the raspberries and confectioners' sugar to a purée in a food processor or blender. Press through a nylon strainer. To make the meringue, sift the cornstarch into a bowl and stir in the superfine sugar. Whisk the egg whites in a large, clean bowl until stiff peaks form. Whisk in the vinegar. Gradually whisk in the cornstarch mixture until stiff and glossy.

Spread the mixture evenly in the prepared pan. Bake in the center of the preheated oven for 20 minutes, then reduce the heat to 225°F/110°C and bake for an additional 25-30 minutes, or until puffed up. Let cool for 15 minutes, then turn out onto nonstick parchment paper.

To make the filling, mix the peaches, raspberries, and 2 tablespoons of the coulis together in a bowl. Whip the sour cream and cream together in a separate bowl until thick. Spread over the meringue. Sprinkle the fruit mixture over the cream, leaving a 1 1/4-inch/3-cm border at one short edge. Using the parchment paper, lift and roll the meringue, starting at the short edge without the border, ending up seam-side down. Lift onto a plate and serve with the remaining coulis.

This cloud of meringue is a dessert to die for—crunchy on the outside and gooey within. The meringue can be made up to 8 hours before being filled, and once assembled, the roulade will keep for up to 2 days in the refrigerator.

CHERRY AND CHOCOLATE MERINGUE

SERVES 4

4 large egg whites

1 cup superfine sugar

1 tsp cornstarch, sifted

1 tsp white wine vinegar

1 tbsp unsweetened cocoa

ready-made semisweet chocolate
  caraque, to decorate

TOPPING

1³/4 cups heavy cream

¹/4 cup confectioners' sugar, sifted

4 tbsp maple syrup

4 tbsp unsalted butter

1 lb/450 g black cherries

A luscious, sticky chocolate
meringue base smothered in cream
and luscious cherries.

Preheat the oven to 275°F/140°C. Line a cookie sheet with nonstick parchment paper.

Whisk the egg whites in a large, clean bowl until stiff peaks form. Gradually whisk in the superfine sugar and continue whisking until very stiff and glossy. Fold in the cornstarch, vinegar, cocoa, and chocolate. Spread onto the cookie sheet to form a 9¹/2-inch/24-cm circle. Bake in the preheated oven for 1¹/2 hours.

Turn off the oven and leave the meringue in the oven for 45 minutes.

To make the topping, whisk the cream and confectioners' sugar together in a bowl until stiff. Cover and let chill in the refrigerator. Pit most of the cherries, reserving a few whole. Melt the maple syrup with the butter in a skillet and stir in the pitted cherries to coat. Let cool.

When the meringue is cold, peel off the parchment paper.

To serve, put the meringue on a dish. Spoon the cream mixture into the center and pile on the cherries, using the whole ones around the edge. Top with the chocolate caraque.

FROSTED **CHOCOLATE** CAKE

SERVES 6

butter, for greasing

4 eggs

generous $1/2$ cup superfine sugar

scant 1 cup all-purpose flour

semisweet chocolate caraque, to
   decorate

CHOCOLATE CREAM

$2/3$ cup heavy cream

$5^{1}/2$ oz/150 g semisweet chocolate,
   broken into pieces

FROSTING

$2^{3}/4$ oz/75 g white chocolate, broken
   into pieces

1 tbsp butter

1 tbsp milk

4 tbsp confectioners' sugar, sifted

Preheat the oven to 350°F/180°C. Grease and base-line an 8-inch/20-cm round springform cake pan. Using a hand-held electric whisk, beat the eggs and superfine sugar together in a large bowl until thick and pale—the mixture should leave a trail when the whisk is lifted.

Sift in the flour and fold in gently with a metal spoon or a palette knife. Pour into the prepared pan and bake in the preheated oven for 35-40 minutes, or until springy to the touch. Let cool slightly in the pan, then transfer to a cooling rack and let cool completely.

Meanwhile, to make the chocolate cream, bring the cream to a boil in a pan, stirring constantly. Add the semisweet chocolate and stir until melted and well combined. Remove from the heat, transfer to a bowl, and let cool. Beat with a wooden spoon until thick.

When the cake is cold, cut horizontally in half. Sandwich the layers together with the chocolate cream. Transfer to a cooling rack.

To make the frosting, melt the white chocolate and butter together in a heatproof bowl set over a pan of barely simmering water, stirring until blended. Whisk in the milk and confectioners' sugar, and continue whisking until cool. Pour the frosting over the cake and spread with a palette knife to coat the top and side. Decorate with chocolate caraque and let the frosting set before serving.

If you can't decide whether you prefer dark chocolate or rich, creamy white chocolate, then this gâteau is definitely for you.

DEVIL'S **FOOD** CAKE

Preheat the oven to 375°F/190°C. Grease and base-line 2 x 8-inch/ 20-cm shallow cake pans. Melt the chocolate in a heatproof bowl set over a pan of barely simmering water. Sift the flour and baking soda together into a bowl.

Cream the butter and sugar together in a separate bowl until pale and fluffy. Beat in the vanilla extract and the eggs, one at a time, beating well after each addition. Add a little flour if the mixture starts to curdle.

Fold the melted chocolate into the mixture until well blended. Gradually fold in the remaining flour, then stir in the buttermilk and boiling water.

Divide the batter between the prepared pans and smooth the surfaces. Bake in the preheated oven for 30 minutes, or until springy to the touch. Let the cakes cool slightly in the pans, then transfer to a cooling rack and let cool completely.

To make the frosting, put all the ingredients in a large heatproof bowl set over a pan of gently simmering water. Using a hand-held electric whisk, beat until thick and soft peaks form. Remove from the heat and beat until cool.

Sandwich the cakes together with some of the frosting. Swirl the remainder over the top and side of the cake. Decorate with candied orange rind.

SERVES 6

1 cup butter, plus extra
    for greasing

3^1/2 oz/100 g semisweet chocolate,
    broken into pieces

scant 1^1/3 cups self-rising flour

1 tsp baking soda

1 lb 2 oz/500 g light brown sugar

1 tsp vanilla extract

3 eggs

^{1}/2 cup buttermilk

scant 1 cup boiling water

candied orange rind, to decorate

FROSTING

generous 1^1/8 cups superfine sugar

2 egg whites

1 tbsp lemon juice

3 tbsp orange juice

This classic melt-in-the-mouth chocolate cake is given a tangy
citrus-flavored frosting in this recipe.

CHOCOLATE **FUDGE** GATEAU

SERVES 10

1 tsp sunflower-seed oil, for oiling

3 oz/85 g semisweet chocolate

1 cup butter, softened

generous 1¹/₈ cups brown sugar

4 eggs, beaten

scant 1⁵/₈ cups self-rising flour

generous ¹/₂ cup ground almonds

1-2 tbsp cooled, boiled water

4 oz/115 g soft vanilla fudge, diced

FROSTING

³/₄ cup butter, softened

2¹/₂ cups confectioners' sugar, sifted

3-4 tbsp light cream

generous ¹/₄ cup light brown sugar

1 tbsp unsweetened cocoa, sifted

TO DECORATE

55 g/2 oz semisweet chocolate, grated

cocoa-dusted truffles

Preheat the oven to 350°F/180°C. Lightly oil and base-line 2 x 8-inch/20-cm shallow cake pans with nonstick parchment paper. Melt the chocolate in a heatproof bowl set over a pan of barely simmering water. Cream the butter and brown sugar together in a bowl until light and fluffy, then gradually add the eggs, beating well and adding a little of the flour after each addition. Gently fold in the melted chocolate and then the remaining flour until combined.

Stir in the ground almonds with the cooled boiled water. Mix to form a soft dropping consistency. Stir in the fudge pieces, then divide between the prepared cake pans and smooth the surfaces.

Bake in the preheated oven for 35–40 minutes, or until springy to the touch. Let the cakes cool slightly in the pans, then transfer to a cooling rack and let cool completely.

To make the frosting, beat the butter in a bowl until soft and creamy, then gradually beat in the confectioners' sugar, adding a little of the cream as the mixture becomes stiff. Add the brown sugar with the cocoa and gently stir. Stir in sufficient of the remaining cream to give a soft, spreadable frosting.

Put the grated chocolate on a sheet of nonstick parchment paper. Cut the cakes horizontally in half and sandwich together with one-third of the frosting. Spread another third around the side, then roll the cake in the grated chocolate. Transfer to a serving plate. Spread the top with the remaining frosting, piping rosettes around the outside edge for an attractive finish. Decorate with the truffles before serving.

This gâteau is absolutely delicious and combines all of the most wickedly delectable ingredients.

RICH CHOCOLATE CAKE

SERVES 10

$^5/_8$ cup butter, preferably unsalted,
   plus extra for greasing

6 oz/175 g semisweet chocolate,
   broken into pieces

scant $^3/_4$ cup superfine sugar

6 eggs, separated

scant 1$^1/_4$ cups all-purpose flour

FROSTING AND FILLING

8 oz/225 g semisweet chocolate,
   broken into pieces

5 tbsp cold strong black coffee

1 cup confectioners' sugar, sifted

6 tbsp good-quality apricot jelly,
   warmed

Preheat the oven to 300°F/ 150°C. Grease and base-line a 9-inch/23-cm round springform cake pan. Melt the chocolate in a heatproof bowl set over a pan of barely simmering water. Cream the butter and generous $^1/_3$ cup of the superfine sugar in a bowl until pale and fluffy. Add the egg yolks and beat well. Add the melted chocolate in a thin stream, beating well. Sift the flour, then fold into the mixture. Whisk the egg whites in a separate large, clean bowl until soft peaks form. Add the remaining superfine sugar and whisk until stiff and glossy. Fold half into the chocolate mixture, then fold in the remainder.

Spoon into the prepared pan and smooth the surface. Bake in the preheated oven for 1-1$^1/_4$ hours, or until a skewer inserted into the center comes out clean. Let the cake cool slightly in the pan, then transfer to a cooling rack and let cool completely.

To make the frosting, melt 6 oz/175 g of the chocolate in a heatproof bowl set over a pan of barely simmering water. Beat in the coffee. Whisk into the confectioners' sugar in a bowl to form a thick frosting. Cut the cake horizontally in half. Sandwich the layers together with the jelly. Invert the cake onto a cooling rack. Spoon over the frosting and spread to coat the top and side. Let set for 5 minutes, letting any excess drip through the rack. Transfer to a serving plate and let set for at least 2 hours. Melt the remaining chocolate and spoon into a pastry bag fitted with a fine plain tip. Pipe "Sachertorte" on the cake top and let set.

PASSION FRUIT ANGEL CAKE

SERVES 8

²/₃ cup all-purpose flour

generous 1³/₈ cups superfine sugar

8 large egg whites

1 tsp cream of tartar

pinch of salt

1 tsp vanilla extract

2 tbsp warm water

FROSTING

4 passion fruit

1¹/₂ cups confectioners' sugar

Angel cake is wonderfully light and airy. A passion fruit frosting makes it even more delicious.

If you do not have an angel cake pan, any other pan can be used.

Preheat the oven to 350°F/180°C. Sift the flour and 2 tablespoons of the superfine sugar together onto a sheet of waxed paper. Put the egg whites in a large, clean bowl and whisk until frothy, then stir in the cream of tartar and salt. Sprinkle in the vanilla extract and warm water and continue whisking until the egg whites are stiff but not dry. Sift in the remaining superfine sugar, 2 tablespoons at a time, whisking well after each addition, until soft peaks form.

Gradually fold in the flour mixture gently. Pour the batter into a nonstick angel cake pan with a funnel—it should be two-thirds full. Bake in the preheated oven for 50-55 minutes until the top is brown and dry to the touch. Invert the pan and leave until the cake is cold. Ease the cake out of the pan with a palette knife and transfer to a serving plate.

To make the frosting, halve the passion fruit and scoop out the pulp into a strainer set over a bowl. Press the juice from the pulp with a wooden spoon. Stir in enough confectioners' sugar to make a frosting with the consistency of heavy cream. Pour the frosting over the cake and let set.

FRUIT AND MARZIPAN CAKE

Line a 9-inch/23-cm round cake pan with waxed paper and grease it thoroughly.

Wash the cherries and pat dry, then halve them. Finely chop the almonds. Mix the dried fruit, peel, nuts, and the lemon and orange rinds together in a bowl. Add half the amaretto and let stand for 1 hour.

Preheat the oven to 350°F/180°C.

Cream the butter and sugar together in a bowl until pale and fluffy. Add the eggs, a little at a time, beating well after each addition. Using a grater, coarsely grate 4 oz/115 g of the marzipan. Add to the soaked fruit with the creamed mixture. Sift the baking powder, cinnamon, and flour together and fold in gently.

Put half the mixture in the prepared cake pan and smooth the surface. Roll out half the remaining marzipan into an 8-inch/20-cm circle and put into the cake pan. Cover with the remaining cake batter. Smooth over, making a slight dip in the center.

Bake in the preheated oven for 1 hour, then reduce the temperature to 325°F/160°C. Bake for an additional 2 hours, then test with a skewer inserted into the center. If the skewer does not come out clean, bake for an additional 30–45 minutes.

Transfer the cake to a cooling rack. Prick the surface of the cake lightly with a fork or skewer. Pour over the remaining amaretto and let the cake cool completely before removing from the pan. Keep the cake covered in waxed paper with a layer of foil until required.

Brush the cake surface with a little beaten egg white. Use the remaining marzipan to make decorations, such as flowers and leaves, and add to the cake, with twisted strands around the base of the cake.

This is a traditional cake for festive occasions. This version includes amaretto, which intensifies its almond flavor and keeps it very moist.

SERVES 8-10

4 oz/115 g candied cherries

scant $^1/_2$ cup whole blanched almonds

2 cups golden raisins

scant $2^1/_2$ cups currants

generous $2^1/_8$ cups raisins

$^2/_3$ cup candied peel

generous $^1/_2$ cup ground almonds

grated rind of 1 lemon

grated rind of 1 orange

5 tbsp amaretto

1 cup unsalted butter, plus extra
   for greasing

generous $1^1/_8$ cups light brown sugar

6 eggs, beaten

2 lb 4 oz/1 kg ready-made marzipan

$1^1/_2$ tsp baking powder

1 tsp ground cinnamon

2 cups all-purpose flour

lightly beaten egg white, for brushing

SERVES 8-10

1 tsp sunflower-seed oil, for oiling

6 oz/175 g semisweet chocolate,
   broken into pieces

2-3 tbsp kirsch or brandy

5 eggs

generous 1^1/$_8$ cups superfine sugar

2 tbsp confectioners' sugar, sifted

FILLING AND DECORATION

1^1/$_2$ cups heavy cream

1 tbsp kirsch or brandy

12 oz/350 g fresh black cherries,
   pitted, or 14 oz/400 g canned
   morello cherries, drained
   and pitted

squares of chocolate, to decorate

CHERRY CHOCOLATE ROLL

Preheat the oven to 375°F/190°C. Oil a 14 x 10-inch/35 x 25-cm jelly roll pan and line with a sheet of nonstick parchment paper.

Melt the chocolate in a heatproof bowl set over a pan of barely simmering water. Add the kirsch and heat gently, stirring until the mixture is smooth. Remove the bowl from the pan and let cool.

Put the eggs and sugar in a large heatproof bowl set over the pan of barely simmering water. Using a hand-held electric whisk, whisk together until thick and pale—the mixture should leave a trail when the whisk is lifted. Remove the bowl from the pan and whisk in the cooled chocolate.

Spoon into the prepared jelly roll pan, then tap the pan lightly on the counter to smooth the surface. Bake in the preheated oven for 20 minutes, or until springy to the touch. Remove from the oven and immediately turn out onto a sheet of nonstick parchment paper sprinkled with the confectioners' sugar. Peel off the lining paper and roll up the cake tightly, encasing the parchment paper. Wrap in a clean dish towel and let cool.

Whip the cream in a bowl until soft peaks form, then stir in the kirsch. Set aside 1-2 tablespoons of the cream. Unroll the cake and spread with the remaining cream to within ^{1}/$_4$ inch/5 mm of the edges. Set aside a few of the cherries for decoration and sprinkle the remainder over the cream. Carefully roll up the cake again and transfer to a serving plate. Decorate the top with small rosettes or small spoonfuls of the reserved cream, the reserved cherries, and squares of chocolate.

Do not worry if the roll cracks when it is rolled up. It has a tendency to do this and it does not detract from the sumptuous taste.

RICH CARROT CAKE

Decorating this moist, rich carrot cake lifts it into the celebration class.

SERVES 10

butter, for greasing

2/3 cup sunflower-seed or corn oil

scant 1 cup golden superfine sugar

4 tbsp plain yogurt

3 eggs, plus 1 egg yolk

1 tsp vanilla extract

1 cup walnut pieces, chopped

6 oz/175 g carrots, grated

1 banana, peeled and mashed

scant 1^5/$_8$ cups all-purpose flour

3 oz/85 g fine oatmeal

1 tsp each of baking soda, baking
    powder, and ground cinnamon

1/2 tsp salt

FROSTING

generous 1/2 cup cream cheese

4 tbsp plain yogurt

3/4 cup confectioners' sugar

1 tsp grated lemon rind

2 tsp lemon juice

TO DECORATE

primroses and violets

1 egg white, lightly beaten

3 tbsp superfine sugar

Preheat the oven to 350°F/180°C. Grease and line a 9-inch/23-cm round cake pan. Beat the oil, sugar, yogurt, eggs, egg yolk, and vanilla extract together in a bowl. Beat in the nuts, carrot, and banana.

Sift the remaining cake ingredients together and gradually beat into the batter. Pour into the prepared pan and smooth the surface. Bake in the preheated oven for 1^1/$_2$ hours, or until firm and a fine skewer inserted into the center comes out clean. Let cool in the pan for 15 minutes, then transfer to a cooling rack and let cool completely.

To make the frosting, beat the cream cheese and yogurt together in a bowl. Sift in the confectioners' sugar and stir in the lemon rind and juice. Spread over the top and side of the cake.

To prepare the decoration, dip the flowers quickly in the beaten egg white, then sprinkle with superfine sugar to cover the surface. Space well apart on nonstick parchment paper. Leave in a warm, dry place for several hours until dry and crisp. Arrange on the cake top.

SUMMER FRUIT TARTLETS

MAKES 12

PIE DOUGH

scant 1¹/₂ cups all-purpose flour, plus
extra for dusting

³/₄ cup confectioners' sugar

generous ¹/₂ cup ground almonds

8 tbsp butter

1 egg yolk

1 tbsp milk

FILLING

1 cup cream cheese

confectioners' sugar, to taste, plus
extra for dusting

12 oz/350 g fresh summer fruits, such
as red currants, blueberries,
raspberries, and small strawberries

The fruit in the tarts could be
brushed with warmed red currant jelly
to make an attractive glaze.

To make the pie dough, sift the flour and confectioners' sugar into a bowl. Stir in the ground almonds. Add the butter and rub in until the mixture resembles bread crumbs. Add the egg yolk and milk and work in with a palette knife, then mix with your fingers until the dough binds together. Wrap the dough in plastic wrap and let chill for 30 minutes.

Preheat the oven to 400°F/200°C. On a floured counter, roll out the dough and use it to line 12 deep tartlet or individual brioche pans. Prick the bases. Press a piece of foil into each tartlet, covering the edges, and bake in the preheated oven for 10-15 minutes, or until light golden brown. Remove the foil and bake for an additional 2-3 minutes. Transfer to a cooling rack to cool.

To make the filling, place the cream cheese and confectioners' sugar in a bowl and mix together. Place a spoonful of filling in each pastry shell and arrange the fruit on top. Dust with sifted confectioners' sugar and serve immediately.

CHOCOLATE AND RASPBERRY TART

SERVES 6

PIE DOUGH

scant 1¹/₄ cups all-purpose flour, plus
extra for dusting

8 tbsp butter, chilled

1 tbsp superfine sugar

1 egg yolk

FILLING

1 lb/450 g fresh raspberries

2 tbsp flower honey

4¹/₂ oz/125 g white chocolate

generous 1 cup mascarpone cheese

²/₃ cup heavy cream, whipped

This is a light, white chocolate tart,
swirled with raspberry sauce and
served with fresh raspberries. It would
be equally delicious made with
strawberries or blueberries.

To make the pie dough, sift the flour into a bowl. Grate in the butter, then rub in with your fingertips until the mixture resembles fine bread crumbs. Stir in the sugar, egg yolk, and enough cold water to form a soft dough. Roll out on a lightly floured counter and use to line an 8-inch/ 20-cm round tart pan. Prick the base all over with a fork and let chill in the refrigerator for 30 minutes.

Preheat the oven to 375°F/190°C. Line the tart shell with baking paper, fill with baking beans, and bake in the preheated oven for 15 minutes. Reduce the temperature to 350°F/180°C, remove the paper and beans and bake for an additional 15-20 minutes. Let cool in the pan, then transfer the tart shell to a serving plate.

Set aside a handful of raspberries, then press the remainder through a nylon strainer into a small pan. Stir in the honey. Bring to a boil and boil until thick, then remove from the heat and let cool completely.

Melt the chocolate in a heatproof bowl set over a pan of barely simmering water. Let cool. Mix with the mascarpone cheese and cream. Swirl in the raspberry sauce to give a marbled effect and spoon into the tart shell. Decorate with the remaining raspberries and serve.

CHOCOLATE PUFF PASTRIES

This is a novel way of serving a
creamy white chocolate parfait in
a crisp pastry "sandwich."
It is the perfect finale to any
dinner-party meal.

For a more elegant version, drizzle a
little melted semisweet chocolate over
the sandwiches or sprinkle with a little
sifted confectioners' sugar.

SERVES 4

3 large egg whites

³/4 cup superfine sugar

5 oz/140 g white chocolate, grated

1³/4 cups whipping cream, whipped

**12 oz/350 g ready-rolled puff pastry,
thawed if frozen**

To make the parfait, beat the egg whites and sugar together in a
heatproof bowl, then set the bowl over a pan of barely simmering water.
Using a hand-held electric whisk, beat until stiff peaks form. Remove
from the heat, add the chocolate, and continue beating until cool. Fold
in the cream.

Spoon the parfait into a shallow rectangular freezerproof container
and freeze for 5-6 hours.

When ready to bake, preheat the oven to 350°F/180°C and line a
cookie sheet with nonstick parchment paper.

Cut the pastry into 8 regular-sized rectangles large enough to
accommodate a slice of the parfait. Transfer the pastry rectangles to
the prepared cookie sheet and top with another cookie sheet, which will
keep the pastry flat but crisp. Bake in the preheated oven for
15 minutes. Transfer to a cooling rack and let cool.

About 20 minutes before you are ready to serve, remove the parfait
from the freezer. When it has softened, cut the parfait into slices and put
each slice between 2 pieces of pastry to make a "sandwich."

HONEY AND LEMON TART

To make the pie dough, put the flour, salt, sugar, and butter in a food processor. Process in short bursts until the mixture resembles fine bread crumbs. Sprinkle over the water and mix to form a smooth dough. Alternatively, put the flour, salt, and sugar in a bowl and rub in the butter with your fingertips. Add the water and mix to form a smooth dough. For the best results, wrap in foil or plastic wrap and let chill in the refrigerator for 30 minutes.

Meanwhile, to make the filling, if using cottage cheese, press the cheese through a strainer into a bowl. Add the honey to the cheese and beat until smooth. Add the eggs, cinnamon, and lemon rind and juice and mix together well.

When ready to bake, preheat the oven to 400°F/200°C. Roll out the dough on a lightly floured counter and use to line a 9-inch/23-cm round fluted tart pan. Transfer to a cookie sheet. Line with parchment paper and fill with baking beans. Bake in the preheated oven for 15 minutes. Remove the paper and beans and bake for an additional 5 minutes, or until the tart base is firm but not browned.

Reduce the oven temperature to 350°F/180°C. Pour the filling into the tart shell and bake in the oven for 30 minutes, or until set. Serve cold, decorated with slices of lemon.

Use a soft cream cheese for this dessert. Cottage cheese, cream cheese, and ricotta are all suitable choices. Choose an aromatic honey such as orange blossom, for a good flavor.

SERVES 8-12

PIE DOUGH

scant $1^5/8$ cups all-purpose flour, plus extra for dusting

pinch of salt

$1^1/2$ tsp superfine sugar

11 tbsp butter, diced and chilled

3-4 tbsp iced water

FILLING

$1^5/8$ cups cottage cheese, cream cheese, or ricotta cheese

6 tbsp honey

3 eggs, beaten

$1/2$ tsp ground cinnamon

grated rind and juice of 1 lemon

lemon slices, to decorate

CHOCOLATE CHERRY GATEAU

Chocolate and cherries is a classic combination. This is the perfect cake for all special occasions.

MAKES ONE 9-INCH/ 23-CM CAKE

3 tbsp butter, preferably unsalted, melted, plus extra for greasing

2 lb 4 oz/1 kg fresh cherries, pitted and halved

generous 1¹/₈ cups superfine sugar

generous ¹/₃ cup cherry brandy

scant 1 cup all-purpose flour

generous ¹/₂ cup unsweetened cocoa

¹/₂ tsp baking powder

4 eggs

4 cups heavy cream

TO DECORATE

grated semisweet chocolate

whole fresh cherries

Preheat the oven to 350°F/180°C. Grease and line a 9-inch/23-cm round springform cake pan. Put the cherries in a pan and add 3 tablespoons of the sugar and the cherry brandy. Simmer for 5 minutes. Strain and set the syrup and cherries aside separately. Sift the flour, cocoa, and baking powder together into a separate bowl.

Put the eggs in a heatproof bowl and beat in all but 2 tablespoons of the remaining sugar. Set the bowl over a pan of barely simmering water. Using a hand-held electric whisk, beat until thickened. Remove from the heat, then gradually fold in the flour mixture and the melted butter. Spoon into the prepared cake pan and smooth the surface. Bake in the preheated oven for 40 minutes. Let cool in the pan.

Turn out the cake and cut horizontally in half. Whip the cream with the remaining sugar until soft peaks form. Spread the syrup over the cut sides of the cake and spread cream on one cut side. Arrange the cherries on the cream and cover with more cream. Cover with the other cake half, syrup side down, then cover the top and side of the cake. Press grated chocolate over the cake and decorate with whole cherries.

MOCHA LAYER CAKE

SERVES 8

butter, for greasing

scant 2 cups self-rising flour

1/4 tsp baking powder

4 tbsp unsweetened cocoa

generous 1/2 cup superfine sugar

2 eggs

2 tbsp corn syrup

2/3 cup sunflower-seed oil

2/3 cup milk

FILLING AND TOPPING

1 tsp instant coffee powder

1 tbsp boiling water

1 1/4 cups heavy cream

2 tbsp confectioners' sugar

TO DECORATE

1 3/4 oz/50 g chocolate shavings

ready-made chocolate caraque

confectioners' sugar, for dusting

A delicious combination of chocolate sponge and a creamy coffee filling.

Preheat the oven to 350°F/180°C. Lightly grease 3 x 7-inch/18-cm shallow cake pans.

Sift the flour, baking powder, and cocoa together into a large bowl. Stir in the superfine sugar. Make a well in the center. Add the eggs, syrup, oil, and milk to the well and gradually beat in with a wooden spoon to form a smooth batter. Divide between the prepared pans.

Bake in the preheated oven for 35–45 minutes, or until springy to the touch. Let cool slightly in the pans, then transfer to a cooling rack and let cool completely.

To make the filling, dissolve the coffee in the boiling water and put in a bowl with the cream and confectioners' sugar. Whip until the cream is just holding its shape. Use half the cream to sandwich the 3 cakes together. Spread the remaining cream over the top and side of the cake. Press the chocolate shavings into the cream around the side of the cake.

Transfer to a serving plate. Lay the chocolate caraque over the top of the cake. Cut a few thin strips of parchment paper and arrange on top of the caraque. Dust with confectioners' sugar, then remove the paper.

WHITE **TRUFFLE** CAKE

SERVES 12

butter, for greasing

1³/₄ oz/50 g white chocolate

2 eggs

¹/₄ cup superfine sugar

¹/₂ cup all-purpose flour

TRUFFLE TOPPING

1¹/₄ cups heavy cream

12 oz/350 g white chocolate,
 broken into pieces

generous 1 cup mascarpone cheese

TO DECORATE

ready-made chocolate caraque

unsweetened cocoa, for dusting

Preheat the oven to 350°F/180°C. Grease and base-line an 8-inch/ 20-cm round springform cake pan. Melt the white chocolate in a heatproof bowl set over a pan of barely simmering water.

Using a hand-held electric whisk, beat the eggs and sugar together in a large bowl until thick and pale—the mixture should leave a trail when the whisk is lifted. Sift the flour and gently fold into the eggs with a metal spoon or palette knife. Add the melted chocolate. Pour the batter into the prepared pan and bake in the preheated oven for 25 minutes, or until springy to the touch. Let cool slightly in the pan, then transfer to a cooling rack and let cool completely. Return the cold cake to the pan.

To make the topping, put the cream in a pan and bring to a boil, stirring constantly. Let cool slightly, then add the white chocolate and stir until melted and combined. Remove from the heat and set aside until almost cool, stirring, then mix in the mascarpone cheese. Pour on top of the cake. Let chill in the refrigerator for 2 hours.

To decorate, pick up the caraque carefully and arrange on the top of the dessert, before dusting with cocoa.

A light white sponge topped with a rich creamy-white chocolate truffle
mixture makes an out-of-this-world treat.

scones, sweet loaves, AND muffins

In an age when technology moves at a staggering rate, what could be more reassuringly old-fashioned than tucking into a scone, muffin, or slab of fruit loaf, just like grandmother would have made? Whether it is a summertime scone spread with preserve and cream, or a fireside toasted round covered with butter, there is a heart-warming recipe here for every palate, both sweet and savory.

SCONES

Preheat the oven to 425°F/220°C. Grease a cookie sheet.

Sift the flour, salt, and baking powder together into a bowl. Rub in the butter with your fingertips until the mixture resembles fine bread crumbs. Stir in the sugar. Make a well in the center and pour in the milk. Quickly mix with a round-bladed knife to form a soft dough.

Turn out the dough onto a lightly floured counter and knead lightly. Roll out to a thickness of about $1/2$ inch/1 cm. Don't be heavy-handed—scones need a light touch. Using a plain $2^1/2$-inch/6-cm cookie cutter, cut out 10-12 circles and transfer to the prepared cookie sheet.

Brush with the milk to glaze and bake in the preheated oven for 10-12 minutes until well risen and golden.

Transfer to a cooling rack and let cool. Split and serve with clotted cream and strawberry jelly.

MAKES 10-12

4 tbsp butter, diced and chilled, plus
   extra for greasing

1 lb/450 g all-purpose flour, plus extra
   for dusting

$1/2$ tsp salt

2 tsp baking powder

2 tbsp superfine sugar

generous 1 cup milk, plus 3 tbsp
   for glazing

TO SERVE

clotted cream

strawberry jelly

Scones are quick to make and are delicious served freshly baked. Scones can be made with or without fruit. Savory scones, made with a little grated cheese, are also popular and can be served with various fillings as a good alternative to sandwiches.

To make Fruit Scones, add 2 oz/55 g mixed dried fruit with the sugar. To make Whole Wheat Scones, use whole wheat flour and omit the sugar. To make Cheese Scones, omit the sugar and fruit and add $1/2$ cup finely grated Cheddar cheese to the mixture with 1 teaspoon mustard.

BUTTERMILK SCONES

Buttermilk makes these scones extra light, and gives them a tangy flavor. Serve with whipped cream and strawberry jelly.

MAKES 8

4 tbsp butter, diced and chilled, plus extra for greasing

generous 2 cups self-rising flour, plus extra for dusting

1 tsp baking powder

pinch of salt

scant ^{1}/4 cup golden superfine sugar

1^1/4 cups buttermilk

2 tbsp milk, for glazing

TO SERVE
whipped cream
strawberry jelly

Preheat the oven to 425°F/220°C. Grease a cookie sheet.

Sift the flour, baking powder, and salt together into a bowl. Rub in the butter with your fingertips until the mixture resembles fine bread crumbs. Stir in the sugar. Make a well in the center and pour in the buttermilk. Quickly mix with a round-bladed knife to form a soft dough.

Turn out the dough onto a lightly floured counter and knead lightly. Roll out to a thickness of 1 inch/2.5 cm. Don't be heavy-handed when rolling the dough-scones need a light touch. Using a 2^1/2-inch/6-cm plain or fluted cookie cutter, cut out 8 circles and transfer to the prepared cookie sheet.

Brush with the milk to glaze and bake in the preheated oven for 12-15 minutes until well risen and golden.

Transfer to a cooling rack and let cool. Split and serve with whipped cream and strawberry jelly.

CHERRY SCONES

Preheat the oven to 425°F/220°C. Grease a cookie sheet.

Sift the flour and salt together into a bowl. Rub in the butter with your fingertips until the mixture resembles fine bread crumbs. Stir in the sugar, cherries, and golden raisins, then add the beaten egg.

Add 2 tablespoons of the milk to the mixture, setting aside 1 tablespoon of the milk for glazing. Quickly mix with a round-bladed knife to form a soft dough.

Turn out the dough onto a lightly floured counter and knead lightly. Roll out to a thickness of $3/4$ inch/2 cm. Don't be heavy-handed–scones need a light touch. Using a 2-inch/5-cm plain or fluted cookie cutter, cut out 8 circles and transfer to the prepared cookie sheet.

Brush with the remaining milk to glaze and bake in the preheated oven for 8–10 minutes until well risen and golden.

Transfer to a cooling rack and let cool. Split, spread generously with butter and serve.

MAKES 8

6 tbsp butter, diced and chilled,
 plus extra for greasing and to serve

scant 1⁵/₈ cups self-rising flour,
 plus extra for dusting

pinch of salt

1 tbsp superfine sugar

3 tbsp candied cherries, chopped

3 tbsp golden raisins

1 egg, lightly beaten

3 tbsp milk

These are an alternative to traditional scones, using sweet candied cherries, which not only create color but add a distinctive flavor. These scones will freeze very successfully, but they are best thawed and eaten within 1 month.

MAKES 10-12

generous 2³/₈ cups all-purpose flour

pinch of salt

¹/₂ oz/15 g fresh yeast

1 tsp superfine sugar

1³/₄ cups tepid milk

butter, for greasing and to serve

TOASTED ROUNDS

Sift the flour and salt together into a bowl. Blend the fresh yeast with the sugar in a small bowl and stir in the milk. Make a well in the flour, pour in the yeast mixture and gradually beat in to form a batter. Continue beating until the batter is light and airy. Cover and let rise in a warm place for 1 hour, or until well risen.

Stir the batter to knock out any air and check the consistency. If it is too thick, add 1 tablespoon water (it should look rather gloopy). Let stand for 10 minutes.

Grease a large skillet and 4 x 3-inch/7.5-cm plain cookie cutters. Heat the skillet over medium heat for 2 minutes. Arrange the cutters in the skillet and spoon in enough batter to come halfway up each cutter. Cook over low heat for 5-6 minutes until small holes begin to appear and the top is starting to dry.

Remove the cutters with a palette knife or an oven mitt. Turn the rounds over (the base should be golden brown) and cook for 1-2 minutes until cooked through.

Remove the toasted rounds with a spatula and keep warm while you cook the remaining batter.

Serve freshly cooked with butter, or if you want to serve them later, let cool and reheat in a toaster or by the fire.

Toasted rounds have always been associated with winter firesides and tea-time, and there is nothing nicer than to sit by a roaring fire with a toasting fork in your hand toasting rounds. Spreading them with lots of butter until it drips through your fingers is also part of the experience. Making them at home is a magical experience as you watch the traditional "bubble" appearance develop.

FUDGE NUT MUFFINS

Chewy pieces of fudge give these muffins a lovely texture and contrast with the crunchiness of the nuts. Store in airtight containers.

MAKES 12

scant 2 cups all-purpose flour

4 tsp baking powder

generous $^3/_8$ cup superfine sugar

6 tbsp crunchy peanut butter

1 egg, beaten

4 tbsp butter, melted

$^3/_4$ cup milk

$5^1/_2$ oz/150 g vanilla fudge, diced

**3 tbsp coarsely chopped
    unsalted peanuts**

Preheat the oven to 400°F/200°C. Line a 12-hole muffin pan with muffin paper cases. Sift the flour and baking powder together into a bowl. Stir in the sugar. Add the peanut butter and mix until the mixture resembles bread crumbs.

Put the egg, butter, and milk in a separate bowl and beat together until blended. Stir into the flour mixture until just blended. Lightly stir in the fudge pieces. Do not overstir the batter—it is fine for it to be a little lumpy.

Spoon the batter evenly into the paper cases. Sprinkle the peanuts on top and bake in the preheated oven for 20-25 minutes until well risen and springy to the touch.

Let the muffins cool slightly in the pan, then serve, or transfer to a cooling rack and let cool completely.

DOUBLE CHOCOLATE MUFFINS

MAKES 12

generous 1³/8 cups all-purpose flour

generous ¹/4 cup unsweetened cocoa,
   plus extra for dusting

1 tbsp baking powder

1 tsp ground cinnamon

¹/2 cup golden superfine sugar

6¹/2 oz/185 g white chocolate,
   broken into pieces

2 eggs

generous ¹/3 cup sunflower-seed oil

1 cup milk

Chocolate-flavored muffins with a
white chocolate frosting are sure to
please children and adults alike.

When stirring the muffin mixture
together, do not over-stir, otherwise
the muffins will be tough. The mixture
should be quite lumpy.

Preheat the oven to 400°F/200°C. Line a 12-hole muffin pan with muffin paper cases. Sift the flour, cocoa, baking powder, and cinnamon together into a large bowl. Stir in the sugar and 4¹/2 oz/125 g of the chocolate.

Put the eggs and oil in a separate bowl and whisk together until frothy, then gradually whisk in the milk. Stir into the flour mixture until just blended. Spoon the batter evenly into the paper cases, filling each three-quarters full.

Bake in the preheated oven for 20 minutes, or until well risen and springy to the touch. Let the muffins cool slightly in the pan, then transfer to a cooling rack and let cool completely.

Melt the remaining chocolate in a heatproof bowl set over a pan of barely simmering water and spread over the tops of the muffins. Let set, then dust the tops with a little cocoa and serve.

APPLE AND CINNAMON MUFFINS

These spicy muffins are quick and easy to make with a few stock ingredients and two apples. The crunchy sugar topping turns them into a real treat.

MAKES 6

²/3 cup whole wheat flour

¹/2 cup all-purpose flour

1¹/2 tsp baking powder

pinch of salt

1 tsp ground cinnamon

¹/4 cup golden superfine sugar

2 small eating apples, peeled, cored, and finely chopped

¹/2 cup milk

1 egg, beaten

4 tbsp butter, melted

TOPPING

12 brown sugar lumps, coarsely crushed

¹/2 tsp ground cinnamon

Preheat the oven to 400°F/200°C. Line 6 holes of a muffin pan with muffin paper cases.

Sift the flours, baking powder, salt, and cinnamon together into a large bowl, then stir in the sugar and apples. Put the milk, egg, and butter in a separate bowl and beat together until blended. Stir into the flour mixture until just blended. Do not overstir the batter—it is fine for it to be a little lumpy.

Spoon the batter evenly into the paper cases. To make the topping, mix the crushed sugar lumps and cinnamon together and sprinkle over the tops of the muffins. Bake in the preheated oven for 20-25 minutes until well risen and springy to the touch. Let the muffins cool slightly in the pan, then serve, or transfer to a cooling rack and let cool.

Work quickly once you have chopped the apple, as the flesh soon starts to brown on exposure to the air.

BLUEBERRY MUFFINS

MAKES 12

scant 1⁵/₈ cups all-purpose flour

1 tsp baking soda

¹/₄ tsp salt

1 tsp ground allspice

generous ¹/₂ cup superfine sugar

3 egg whites

3 tbsp margarine

²/₃ cup thick plain or blueberry-
    flavored yogurt

1 tsp vanilla extract

4 oz/115 g fresh blueberries

Another way to test that your muffins
are cooked is to insert a toothpick into
the center of one of the muffins. If it
comes out clean, they are cooked. If
not, return the muffins to the oven
and bake for a little longer.

Preheat the oven to 375°F/190°C. Line a 12-hole muffin pan with 12
muffin paper cases. Sift the flour, baking soda, salt, and half the allspice
together into a large bowl. Add 6 tablespoons of the sugar and mix
together well.

Lightly whisk the egg whites together with a fork in a separate bowl.
Add the margarine, yogurt, and vanilla extract and beat together until
blended, then stir in the blueberries until thoroughly mixed. Stir into the
flour mixture until just blended. Do not overstir the batter—it is fine for
it to be a little lumpy.

Spoon the batter evenly into the paper cases, filling each about two-
thirds full.

Mix the remaining sugar with the remaining allspice, then sprinkle
over the tops of the muffins. Bake in the preheated oven for
25 minutes, or until well risen and springy to the touch.

Let the muffins cool slightly in the pan, then serve, or transfer to a
cooling rack and let cool completely.

ITALIAN TOMATO MUFFINS

Peel the tomatoes (see below), halve, then scoop out the seeds with a teaspoon and discard. Chop the tomatoes finely and set aside.

Preheat the oven to 400°F/200°C. Lightly oil a 12-hole muffin pan or line with 12 muffin paper cases. Sift the flour, baking powder, and salt together into a large bowl. Add the cornmeal and mix together well.

Lightly whisk the egg and milk together with a fork in a separate bowl. Add the tomatoes, then the garlic, basil, and parsley and mix together well. Stir into the flour mixture until just blended. Do not overstir the batter—it is fine for it to be a little lumpy.

Spoon the muffin batter evenly into the muffin holes or the paper cases, filling each about two-thirds full.

Bake in the preheated oven for 20 minutes, or until well risen and springy to the touch.

Let the muffins cool slightly in the pan, then serve, or transfer to a cooling rack and let cool completely.

MAKES 12

10¹/₂ oz/300 g Italian plum tomatoes

oil, for oiling (optional)

1 cup all-purpose flour

2 tbsp baking powder

¹/₂ tsp salt

1 cup fine cornmeal

1 egg, lightly beaten

1¹/₄ cups milk

1 garlic clove, crushed

1 tbsp chopped fresh basil

1¹/₂ tsp chopped fresh parsley

To peel tomatoes, bring a kettle of water to a boil. Put the tomatoes in a heatproof bowl, then pour over enough boiling water to cover. Let soak for about 3 minutes, then remove with a slotted spoon and let cool slightly. When the tomatoes are cool enough to handle, gently pierce the skins with the point of a knife. Remove and discard the skins.

CHEESE MUFFINS

MAKES 10

scant 1 cup self-rising flour

1 tbsp baking powder

1 tsp salt

generous 1 cup fine cornmeal

1³/8 cups grated sharp
   Cheddar cheese

4 tbsp butter, melted

2 eggs, beaten

1 garlic clove, crushed

1¹/4 cups milk

Preheat the oven to 400°F/200°C. Line 10 holes of a 12-hole muffin pan with muffin paper cases. Sift the flour, baking powder, and salt together into a bowl. Stir in the cornmeal and 1 cup of the cheese.

Put the butter, eggs, garlic, and milk in a separate bowl and mix together well. Stir into the flour mixture until just blended. Do not overstir the batter—it is fine for it to be a little lumpy.

Spoon the batter evenly into the paper cases, sprinkle over the remaining cheese, and bake in the preheated oven for 20-25 minutes until well risen and springy to the touch. Let the muffins cool slightly in the pan, then serve, or transfer to a cooling rack and let cool.

Cornmeal, or polenta, used to be difficult to find, but it is now widely available in most major supermarkets and health-food stores.

HAM AND LEEK MUFFINS

Cooked bacon works as well as ham in these muffins. You can also replace some or all of the Cheddar cheese with a smoked cheese for an added smoky flavor.

MAKES 12

2 tbsp vegetable oil, plus extra for oiling (optional)

1 leek, trimmed and finely chopped

2 cups all-purpose flour

2 tsp baking powder

1/2 tsp baking soda

1 egg, lightly beaten

1 1/4 cups thick strained plain yogurt

4 tbsp butter, melted

1 oz/25 g Cheddar cheese, grated

1 oz/25 g fresh chives, finely snipped

5 1/2 oz/150 g cooked ham, chopped

Preheat the oven to 400°F/200°C. Line a 12-hole muffin pan with a dozen muffin paper cases.

Heat the oil in a skillet over low heat. Add the leek and cook, stirring, for 2 minutes, or until the leaks are soft. Remove from the heat and let cool.

Sift the flour, baking powder, and baking soda together into a large bowl. Lightly mix the egg, yogurt, and butter together in a separate bowl. Add the cheese, chives, leek, and half the chopped ham and mix together well. Stir into the flour mixture until just blended. Do not overstir the batter—it is fine for it to be a little lumpy.

Spoon the muffin batter evenly into the muffin holes or the paper cases, filling each about two-thirds full. Sprinkle over the remaining chopped ham.

Bake in the preheated oven for 20 minutes, or until well risen and springy to the touch. Let the muffins cool slightly in the pan, then serve, or transfer to a cooling rack and let cool completely.

SOUR CREAM MUFFINS WITH CHIVES

MAKES 12

oil, for oiling (optional)

2 cups all-purpose flour

2 tsp baking powder

1/2 tsp baking soda

1 oz/25 g Cheddar cheese, grated

1 1/4 oz/35 g fresh chives, finely
  snipped, plus extra to garnish

1 egg, lightly beaten

scant 1 cup sour cream

generous 1/3 cup plain yogurt

4 tbsp butter, melted

Preheat the oven to 400°F/200°C. Lightly oil a 12-hole muffin pan or line with 12 muffin paper cases.

Sift the flour, baking powder, and baking soda together into a large bowl. Add the cheese and chives and mix together well. Lightly mix the egg, sour cream, yogurt, and butter together in a separate bowl. Stir into the flour mixture until just blended. Do not overstir the batter—it is fine for it to be a little lumpy.

Spoon the muffin batter evenly into the muffin holes or the paper cases, filling each about two-thirds full. Sprinkle over some extra chives to garnish.

Bake in the preheated oven for 20 minutes, or until well risen and springy to the touch. Let the muffins cool slightly in the pan, then serve, or transfer to a cooling rack and let cool completely.

These muffins are deliciously creamy and a real treat for any picnic, buffet, or lunch box. For extra flavor, try stirring 2 tablespoons finely chopped scallion into the batter when you add the chives.

SPICY FRUIT BREAD

Breads are traditionally made using yeast and are flavored with fruits and spices. Today, some breads are made not with yeast but using baking soda or baking powder as a raising agent, but the original recipe using yeast is the best. Serve in thin slices spread with butter.

MAKES 1 LOAF

butter, for greasing

3/4 cup milk

4 tsp active dry yeast

generous 1/2 cup light brown sugar

1 lb/450 g white bread flour, plus extra
   for dusting

1/2 tsp salt

8 tbsp butter

10 oz/280 g mixed dried fruit, such as
   golden raisins, currants, and raisins

1/3 cup candied peel

1 tsp ground allspice

1 egg, beaten

Grease a 2-lb/900-g loaf pan.

Warm the milk in a pan until tepid and add the yeast with 1 teaspoon of the sugar. Mix well and leave in a warm place for 15 minutes until frothy. Sift the flour and salt together into a bowl. Rub in the butter with your fingertips until the mixture resembles fine bread crumbs. Stir in the remaining sugar, dried fruit, candied peel, and allspice. Add the egg and the yeast mixture and mix to form a soft dough.

Turn out the dough onto a lightly floured counter and knead for 5-10 minutes, or until smooth and elastic. Return the dough to the bowl, cover with plastic wrap and let rise in a warm place for 1-1 1/2 hours until doubled in size.

Turn out the dough again and knead lightly. Shape into a rectangle the length of the pan and 3 times the width. Fold the dough lengthwise into 3 and put in the pan with the join underneath. Cover and let prove in a warm place for 30-40 minutes until it has risen above the pan. Preheat the oven to 375ºF/190ºC.

Bake toward the bottom of the preheated oven for 30 minutes. Turn the loaf around and cover the top with foil if it is getting too brown. Bake for an additional 30 minutes, or until the loaf sounds hollow when tapped on the base.

Transfer to a cooling rack and let cool completely. Cut into slices and serve.

GINGER MARMALADE LOAF

Preheat the oven to 350°F/180°C. Grease and line a 2-lb/900-g loaf pan.

Put 1 tablespoon of the marmalade in a small pan and set aside. Put the remaining marmalade in a bowl with the butter, sugar, and eggs. Sift in the flour, baking powder, and ginger and beat together until smooth. Stir in three-quarters of the nuts.

Spoon the batter into the prepared pan and smooth the surface. Sprinkle with the remaining nuts. Bake in the preheated oven for 1 hour, or until well risen and a skewer inserted into the center of the loaf comes out clean.

Leave in the pan for 10 minutes, then transfer to a cooling rack and let cool. Warm the reserved marmalade over low heat, then brush over the warm loaf. Cut into slices and serve.

MAKES 1 LOAF

3/4 cup butter, softened, plus extra
   for greasing
4 1/2 oz/125 g ginger marmalade
scant 1 cup light brown sugar
3 eggs, beaten
scant 1 5/8 cups self-rising flour
1/2 tsp baking powder
1 tsp ground ginger
3/4 cup pecans, coarsely chopped

Ginger marmalade gives a wonderful
flavor to this moist, sticky bread,
which is very quick to prepare.

BANANA AND **CHOCOLATE** BREAD

This is a good loaf to make when you have some overripe bananas in the fruit bowl. It will need to be eaten quickly.

MAKES 1 LOAF

8 tbsp butter, softened, plus extra
for greasing

2 ripe bananas, peeled and mashed

3/8 cup golden superfine sugar

2 eggs

generous 1³/8 cup self-rising flour

generous 1/4 cup unsweetened cocoa

1 tsp baking powder

2 tbsp milk

generous 1/2 cup semisweet
chocolate chips

Preheat the oven to 350°F/180°C. Grease and line a 2-lb/900-g loaf pan.

Mix the bananas, butter, sugar, and eggs together in a bowl. Sift in the flour, cocoa, and baking powder. Beat until smooth, adding enough milk to give a thick dropping consistency. Stir in the chocolate chips.

Spoon the mixture into the prepared pan and smooth the surface. Bake in the preheated oven for 50-60 minutes until well risen and a skewer inserted into the center comes out clean. Leave in the pan for 5 minutes, then transfer to a cooling rack and let cool completely. Serve in slices, with or without butter.

You can mix the ingredients in a food processor, then stir in the chocolate chips by hand.

CHOCOLATE ORANGE BREAD

MAKES 2 LOAVES, EACH SERVING 6

11 tbsp butter, softened, plus extra
    for greasing

2³/4 oz/75 g semisweet chocolate,
    broken into pieces

generous 1¹/4 cups golden superfine
    sugar

5 large eggs, beaten

generous 1 cup all-purpose flour

2 tsp baking powder

pinch of salt

grated rind of 2 oranges

This recipe makes two delicious
chocolate-marbled loaves—one to eat
now and one to freeze for another day.

Preheat the oven to 350°F/180°C. Grease and line 2 x 1-lb/450-g loaf pans.

Melt the chocolate in a large heatproof bowl set over a pan of barely simmering water. Remove from the heat.

Cream the butter and sugar together in a separate bowl until light and fluffy. Gradually add the eggs, a little at a time, beating well after each addition. Sift the flour, baking powder, and salt together and gently fold into the creamed mixture. Transfer one-third of the mixture to the melted chocolate and stir together. Stir the orange rind into the remaining mixture. Divide half the orange mixture between the prepared loaf pans and spread each into an even layer.

Drop tablespoonfuls of the chocolate mixture on top, dividing it between the 2 pans, but do not spread out. Add the remaining orange mixture to the 2 pans. Using a knife, gently swirl the 2 mixtures together to give a marbled effect. Bake in the preheated oven for 35–40 minutes until a skewer inserted into the center of each loaf comes out clean. Let the loaves cool in the pans for 10 minutes, then transfer to a cooling rack and let cool completely.

DATE AND HONEY LOAF

This bread is full of good things—chopped dates, sesame seeds, and honey. Toast thick slices and spread with cream cheese for a light snack.

MAKES 1 LOAF

butter, for greasing

scant 2 cups white bread flour, plus extra for dusting

1/2 cup whole wheat bread flour

1/2 tsp salt

1 1/2 tsp active dry yeast

scant 1 cup tepid water

3 tbsp sunflower-seed oil

3 tbsp honey

3 oz/85 g pitted dates, chopped

2 tbsp sesame seeds

butter or cream cheese, to serve

Grease a 2-lb/900-g loaf pan.

Sift the flours and salt together into a large bowl, then stir in the yeast. Make a well in the center. Add the water, oil, and honey to the well and mix to form a dough.

Turn out the dough onto a lightly floured counter and knead for 5–10 minutes, or until smooth and elastic.

Transfer the dough to a greased bowl, cover, and let rise in a warm place for 1 hour, or until doubled in size.

Turn out the dough again and knead in the dates and sesame seeds. Shape the dough and put in the prepared pan. Cover and let prove in a warm place for 30 minutes, or until springy to the touch. Preheat the oven to 425°F/220°C.

Bake the loaf in the preheated oven for 30 minutes, or until it sounds hollow when tapped on the base.

Transfer the loaf to a cooling rack and let cool completely. Serve cut into thick slices with butter or cream cheese.

MAKES 10-12

4 tbsp butter, melted, plus extra for
 greasing

1¼ cups milk

4 tsp active dry yeast

generous ¼ cup superfine sugar

1 lb/450 g white bread flour, plus extra
 for dusting

1 tsp salt

1 tsp ground allspice

scant 1 cup currants

⅛ cup candied peel, chopped

1 egg, beaten

sugar glaze made from 2 tbsp sugar
 blended with 2 tbsp warm milk

Toasted bread is the basis of a
traditional afternoon tea. It is usually
halved, toasted, and then served with
butter and preserve.

TOASTED BREAD

Grease 2 cookie sheets.

Warm the milk in a pan until just tepid and add the yeast with 1 teaspoon of the sugar. Mix well and leave in a warm place for 15 minutes until frothy.

Sift the flour, salt, and allspice together into a large bowl. Stir in the currants, candied peel, and the remaining sugar. Make a well in the center. Add the yeast mixture, butter, and egg to the well and mix using a wooden spoon at first and then by hand to form a dough.

Turn out the dough onto a lightly floured counter and knead for 5-10 minutes, or until smooth and elastic.

Return the dough to the bowl, cover with plastic wrap, and let rise in a warm place for 40-45 minutes, or until doubled in size.

Turn out the dough again and knead lightly. Cut into 10-12 equal pieces and shape each piece into a bun.

Transfer the buns to the prepared cookie sheets, cover with clean, damp dish towels or large plastic bags, and let prove in a warm place for 30-40 minutes. Preheat the oven to 425ºF/220ºC.

Bake in the preheated oven for 18-20 minutes until golden brown. Transfer to a cooling rack and brush with the sugar glaze while still hot.

sweet breads
AND *buns*

Whether creating a true French-style breakfast, or a high tea spread, sweet yeast breads or buns deserve a place at the table. From Chocolate Croissants to Brioche, Cinnamon Swirls to Chocolate Bread, this section contains a diverse range of baked delights with a rich variety of textures. Here, sticky sweet buns made with yeast—such as that old classic, the Fruity Bun—rub shoulders with doughy snacks like Doughnut Twists, and fruity breads such as Tropical Fruit Bread with Crown Loaf. As if that were not enough to keep you kneading, there is even a recipe for German Fruit Bread—a more unusual take on a traditional sweet yeast bread.

ORANGE AND CURRANT BRIOCHES

Grease 12 individual brioche molds. Sift the flour and salt together into a warmed bowl. Stir in the yeast, sugar, raisins, and orange rind. Make a well in the center. Mix the water, eggs, and butter together and add to the well. Mix to form a soft dough.

Turn out the dough onto a lightly floured counter and knead for 5–10 minutes, or until smooth and elastic. Put the dough in an oiled bowl, cover with plastic wrap, and let rise in a warm place for 1 hour, or until doubled in size.

Turn out the dough again, knead lightly for 1 minute, then roll into a sausage shape. Cut into 12 equal pieces. Shape three-quarters of each piece into a ball and transfer to the prepared molds. With a floured finger, press an indentation in the center of each. Shape the remaining pieces of dough into little plugs and press one into each indentation.

Put the molds on a cookie sheet, cover lightly with oiled plastic wrap,

and leave in a warm place until the dough comes almost to the top of the molds. Preheat the oven to 425°F/220°C.

Brush the brioches with beaten egg. Bake in the preheated oven for 15 minutes, or until golden brown. Serve warm with butter.

MAKES 12

4 tbsp butter, melted, plus extra
for greasing and to serve

1^1/$_2$ cups white bread flour, plus extra
for dusting

^{1}/$_2$ tsp salt

1^1/$_2$ tsp active dry yeast

1 tbsp golden superfine sugar

generous ^{1}/$_3$ cup raisins

grated rind of 1 orange

2 tbsp tepid water

2 eggs, beaten

oil, for oiling

beaten egg, for glazing

Brioche is a light, rich French bread that can be made as one large loaf
or small buns. They are usually served with coffee for breakfast.
If you do not have brioche molds, use a muffin pan instead.

BREAKFAST BRIOCHE

SERVES 6-8

oil, for oiling

1¹/₂ cups white bread flour,
    plus extra for dusting

¹/₂ tsp salt

1¹/₂ tsp active dry yeast

1 tbsp superfine sugar

2 eggs, lightly beaten

2 tbsp tepid milk

4 tbsp butter, melted

GLAZE

1 egg yolk

1 tbsp milk or water

Oil a standard-sized brioche mold.

Sift the flour and salt together into a warmed bowl. Sir in the yeast and sugar. Make a well in the center. Mix the eggs, milk, and butter together and add to the well. Mix to form a dough.

Turn out the dough onto a lightly floured counter and knead for 5-10 minutes, or until smooth and elastic. Put the dough in an oiled bowl, cover with plastic wrap, and let rise in a warm place for 1 hour, or until doubled in size.

Turn out the dough again and knead lightly for 1 minute. Slice off one-quarter of the dough, wrap in oiled plastic wrap, and set aside. Knead the large piece of dough lightly and shape into a ball. Transfer to the prepared mold. With a floured finger, make an indentation in the top or cut a cross with a sharp knife.

Unwrap and lightly knead the reserved dough, shape into a circle, then elongate slightly to a rough pear shape. Put the pear-shaped dough on top of the larger ball of dough, narrow end downward. Cover with lightly oiled plastic wrap, and let prove in a warm place for 1 hour. Preheat the oven to 425°F/220°C.

Meanwhile, to make the glaze, lightly beat the egg yolk with the milk.

Brush the glaze over the top of the brioche. Bake in the preheated oven for 40-45 minutes until risen and golden brown. Transfer to a cooling rack and let cool. Serve warm or cold.

Margarine should never be used when making brioche. Because such a large amount of butter is used, the brioche dough can be successfully frozen.

CHOCOLATE CROISSANTS

Oil 2 cookie sheets. Sift the flour and salt together into a warmed bowl. Stir in the yeast, sugar, and milk powder. Dice 2 tablespoons of the butter and rub into the flour mixture with your fingertips until the mixture resembles bread crumbs. Make a well in the center. Add the water to the well and mix to form a dough.

Turn out the dough onto a lightly floured counter and knead for 5-10 minutes, or until smooth and elastic. Put into an oiled bowl, cover with plastic wrap, and let rise in a warm place for 1 hour, or until doubled in size. Shape the remaining butter into a rectangle 3/4 inch/2 cm thick.

Turn out the dough again and knead lightly for 1 minute. Shape into a ball and cut a cross in the center halfway down through the dough. Roll out the edges of the dough, leaving the cross intact. Put the rectangle of butter in the center and fold the rolled-out edges over it, pressing to seal. Roll out the dough again into a long rectangle. With the short sides facing you, fold the top one-third of the dough down to cover the middle third, then fold the bottom third up and over the top. Press down with the rolling pin to seal the edges. Wrap the dough in oiled plastic wrap and chill in the refrigerator for 20 minutes. Repeat twice more, rolling from the left-hand edge each time, and finally chill for 30 minutes.

Roll out the dough into a rectangle 21 x 12 inches/53 x 30 cm. Cut lengthwise into 3 strips, then widthwise to make 9 equal rectangles. Put a few chocolate pieces on the short end of each rectangle. To make the glaze, beat the egg yolk with the milk. Brush some of the glaze around the edges of the rectangles. Roll up each rectangle to enclose the chocolate. Seal the edges. Transfer to the prepared cookie sheets, seam-side down. Cover with oiled plastic wrap and let prove in a warm place for 30 minutes. Preheat the oven to 400°F/200°C.

Brush the tops of the pastries with the remaining glaze. Bake in the preheated oven for 15 minutes, or until golden. Transfer to a cooling rack to cool. Serve warm.

MAKES 9

oil, for oiling

1⁵/₈ cups white bread flour, plus extra
  for dusting

1/2 tsp salt

1¹/₂ tsp active dry yeast

1 tbsp superfine sugar

2 tbsp skim milk powder

⁵/₈ cup butter, plus extra for greasing

1/2 cup tepid water

8 oz/225 g semisweet chocolate,
  broken into pieces

GLAZE

1 egg yolk

1 tsp milk

A butter-rich flaky exterior
encases a dark chocolate center in
these classic French pastries, which are
divine when freshly baked.

DOUBLE CHOCOLATE SWIRLS

These rich, chocolate buns are very quick to make for breakfast because the dough is prepared the night before.

MAKES 24

1 lb 5 oz/600 g white bread flour, plus extra for dusting

1/2 tsp salt

1 tsp ground cinnamon

1/6 oz/7 g active dry yeast

generous 1/2 cup superfine sugar

6 tbsp unsalted butter, melted and slightly cooled

2 large eggs, beaten, plus 1 egg, beaten, for glazing

1 1/4 cups milk

oil, for oiling

6 tbsp chocolate hazelnut spread

7 oz/200 g milk chocolate, chopped

Sift the flour, salt, and cinnamon together into a large warmed bowl. Stir in the yeast and sugar. Make a well in the center. Mix the butter, the 2 eggs, and milk together and add to the well. Mix to form a soft dough.

Turn out onto a lightly floured counter and knead for 10 minutes, or until smooth and elastic. Put into a large floured bowl, cover with plastic wrap, and let rise in a warm place for 8 hours or overnight.

When you are ready to bake, preheat the oven to 425°F/220°C. Lightly oil 2 cookie sheets. Turn out the dough again and knead lightly for 1 minute. Cut the dough into 4 equal pieces. Roll out each piece into a rectangle about 1-inch/2.5-cm thick. Spread each rectangle with the chocolate hazelnut spread and sprinkle with the chopped chocolate. Roll up each piece like a jelly roll, then cut into 6 pieces.

Transfer each swirl, cut-side down, to the prepared cookie sheets and brush each one well with the beaten egg to glaze. Bake in the preheated oven for 20 minutes. Serve warm.

CROWN LOAF

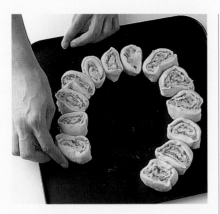

Grease a cookie sheet. Sift the flour and salt together into a warmed bowl. Stir in the yeast. Rub in the butter with your fingertips until the mixture resembles bread crumbs. Add the milk and egg and mix to form a dough.

Put the dough in a greased bowl, cover with plastic wrap, and let rise in a warm place for 40 minutes, or until doubled in size.

Turn out the dough onto a lightly floured counter and knead lightly for 1 minute. Roll out into a rectangle 12 x 9 inches/30 x 23 cm.

To make the filling, cream the butter and brown sugar together in a bowl until light and fluffy. Stir in the nuts, ginger, candied peel, and rum.

Spread the filling over the dough, leaving a 1-inch/2.5-cm border all around. Roll up, starting from one long edge, and press down to seal. Cut into 2-inch/5-cm thick slices and arrange in a circle on the prepared cookie sheet with the slices just touching. Cover and let prove in a warm place for 30 minutes. Preheat the oven to 375°F/190°C.

Bake in the oven for 20–30 minutes, or until golden. Meanwhile, mix the confectioners' sugar with the lemon juice to form a thin frosting.

Let the loaf cool slightly before drizzling with the frosting. Let the frosting set slightly before serving.

MAKES 1 LOAF

2 tbsp butter, diced, plus extra
    for greasing

1¹/2 cups white bread flour, plus extra
    for dusting

¹/2 tsp salt

1¹/2 tsp active dry yeast

¹/2 cup tepid milk

1 egg, lightly beaten

cup confectioners' sugar

2 tbsp lemon juice

FILLING

4 tbsp butter, softened

¹/4 cup light brown sugar

2 tbsp chopped hazelnuts

1 tbsp chopped preserved ginger

generous ¹/4 cup candied peel

1 tbsp dark rum or brandy

This is a rich, sweet bread combining alcohol, nuts, and fruit in a decorative wreath shape. It is ideal for serving at Christmas.

CINNAMON SWIRLS

Grease a 9-inch/23-cm square baking pan.

Sift the flour and salt together into a warmed bowl. Stir in the yeast. Rub in the butter with your fingertips until the mixture resembles bread crumbs. Add the milk and egg and mix to form a dough.

Shape the dough into a ball, then put in a greased bowl, cover with plastic wrap, and let rise in a warm place for 40 minutes, or until doubled in size.

Turn out the dough on a lightly floured counter and knead lightly for 1 minute. Roll out into a rectangle 12 x 9 inches/30 x 23 cm.

To make the filling, cream the butter, cinnamon, and brown sugar together in a bowl until light and fluffy.

Spread the filling over the dough rectangle, leaving a 1-inch/2.5-cm border all around. Sprinkle the currants evenly over the top. Roll up, starting from one long edge, and press down to seal. Cut into 12 slices. Arrange in the prepared pan. Cover and let prove in a warm place for 30 minutes. Preheat the oven to 375°F/190°C.

Bake the buns in the preheated oven for 20–30 minutes, or until well risen. Brush with the syrup and let cool slightly before serving.

MAKES 12

2 tbsp butter, diced, plus extra
   for greasing
1¹/₂ cups white bread flour, plus extra
   for dusting
¹/₂ tsp salt
1¹/₂ tsp active dry yeast
¹/₂ cup tepid milk
1 egg, lightly beaten
2 tbsp maple syrup

FILLING
4 tbsp butter, softened
2 tsp ground cinnamon
¹/₄ cup light brown sugar
generous ¹/₃ cup currants

These cinnamon-flavored buns are delicious if they are served warm a few minutes after they come out of the oven.

APRICOT AND WALNUT BREAD

SERVES 12

4 tbsp butter, diced, plus
   extra for greasing

generous 2$\frac{1}{8}$ cups white bread flour,
   plus extra for dusting

$\frac{1}{2}$ tsp salt

1 tsp golden superfine sugar

2 tsp active dry yeast

$\frac{2}{3}$ cup no-soak dried apricots,
   chopped

generous $\frac{1}{3}$ cup chopped walnuts

$\frac{2}{3}$ cup tepid milk

generous $\frac{1}{4}$ cup tepid water

1 egg, beaten

oil, for oiling

TOPPING

$\frac{3}{4}$ cup confectioners' sugar

walnut halves

Serve this fruit bread freshly made, sliced and buttered, or leave it whole and invite guests to break off tasty morsels with their hands.

As an alternative to apricots, you can substitute candied cherries, dried cranberries, or dates.

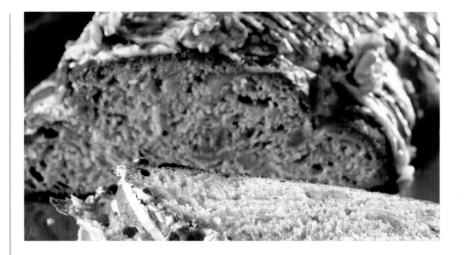

Grease and flour a cookie sheet. Sift the flour and salt together into a warmed bowl. Stir in the superfine sugar and yeast. Rub in the butter with your fingertips until the mixture resembles bread crumbs. Stir in the apricots and walnuts. Make a well in the center. Mix the milk, water, and egg together and add to the well. Mix to form a soft dough. Turn out the dough onto a lightly floured counter and knead for 10 minutes, or until smooth and elastic. Put in an oiled bowl, cover with oiled plastic wrap, and let rise in a warm place for 2–3 hours, or until doubled in size.

Turn out the dough again and knead lightly for 1 minute. Cut into 5 equal pieces and roll each into a rope 12 inches/30 cm long. Plait 3 ropes together, pinching the ends to seal. Transfer to the prepared cookie sheet. Twist the remaining 2 ropes together and put on top. Cover with oiled plastic wrap and let prove in a warm place for 1–2 hours, or until doubled in size. Preheat the oven to 425°F/220°C.

Bake the bread in the preheated oven for 10 minutes. Reduce the heat to 375°F/190°C and bake for an additional 20 minutes. Transfer to a cooling rack to cool. Sift the confectioners' sugar into a bowl, stir in enough water to make a thin frosting, and drizzle over the loaf. Decorate with walnut halves and serve.

MAKES 12

5¹/2 tbsp butter, melted, plus extra
    for greasing

1 lb 2 oz/500 g white bread flour, plus
    extra for dusting

¹/2 tsp salt

2 tsp ground allspice

1 tsp ground nutmeg

1 tsp ground cinnamon

1¹/2 tsp active dry yeast

¹/4 cup golden superfine sugar

finely grated rind of 1 lemon

scant 1¹/4 cups currants

¹/2 cup candied peel

1 egg

about 1 cup tepid milk

CROSSES

generous ¹/3 cup all-purpose flour

2 tbsp butter, diced

GLAZE

3 tbsp milk

3 tbsp golden superfine sugar

FRUITY BUNS

Grease a cookie sheet. Sift the flour, salt, allspice, nutmeg, and cinnamon together into a large warmed bowl. Stir in the yeast, sugar, lemon rind, currants, and candied peel. Make a well in the center. Mix the butter, egg, and milk together and add to the well. Mix to form a soft dough, adding a little more milk if necessary. Turn out the dough onto a lightly floured counter and knead for 10 minutes, or until smooth and elastic. Put the dough in a lightly greased bowl, cover with plastic wrap, and let rise in a warm place for 1¹/2–2 hours, or until doubled in size.

Turn out the dough again and knead lightly for 1 minute. Cut the dough into 12 equal pieces and shape each piece into a ball. Transfer to the prepared cookie sheet and flatten slightly. Cover loosely with greased plastic wrap, and let prove in a warm place for 45 minutes, or until doubled in size. Preheat the oven to 425°F/220°C.

To make the crosses, sift the flour into a bowl. Rub in the butter with your fingertips until the mixture resembles bread crumbs. Stir in a little cold water, about 1 tablespoon, and mix to form a dough. Cut the dough into 24 equal pieces and form into strips about 7 inches/18 cm long.

To make the glaze, gently heat the milk and sugar in a small pan until the sugar has dissolved. Brush a little glaze over the buns, then form crosses with the dough strips. Bake in the preheated oven for 15–20 minutes until golden. Brush with the remaining glaze and bake for another 1 minute. Transfer to a cooling rack to cool.

There is nothing more tempting than the aroma of spicy fruity buns
straight from the oven.

ROLLED **FRUIT** BUNS

Grease a 7-inch/18-cm square cake pan. Sift the flour and salt together into a warmed bowl, then stir in the yeast and superfine sugar. Rub in the butter with your fingertips until the mixture resembles bread crumbs. Make a well in the center. Mix the milk and egg together and add to the well. Mix to form a soft dough. Turn out the dough on to a lightly floured counter and knead for 5–10 minutes, or until smooth and elastic. Put in an oiled bowl, cover with plastic wrap, and let rise in a warm place for 1 hour, or until doubled in size.

Turn out the dough again and knead lightly for 1 minute. Roll out into a rectangle 12 x 9 inches/30 x 23 cm.

To make the filling, mix the brown sugar, dried fruit, and allspice together in a bowl. Spread the dough with the butter and sprinkle the fruit mixture on top. Roll up, starting from one long edge. Cut into 9 slices and arrange, cut-side up, in the prepared pan. Cover with oiled plastic wrap and let prove in a warm place for 45 minutes. Preheat the oven to 375°F/190°C.

Bake the buns in the preheated oven for 30 minutes, or until golden. Let cool in the pan for 10 minutes, then transfer, in one piece, to a cooling rack and let cool completely. Sift the confectioners' sugar into a bowl and stir in enough water to make a thin glaze. Brush over the buns and let set. Pull the buns apart to serve.

MAKES 9

2 tbsp butter, diced, plus extra
   for greasing
1 1/2 cups white bread flour, plus extra
   for dusting
1/2 tsp salt
1 1/2 tsp active dry yeast
1 tsp golden superfine sugar
1/2 cup tepid milk
1 egg, beaten
oil, for oiling
3/4 cup confectioners' sugar

FILLING
generous 1/2 cup packed brown sugar
4 oz/115 g luxury mixed dried fruit
1 tsp ground allspice
4 tbsp butter, softened

These sweet and sticky buns, with a hint of spice, are irresistible. A perfect treat to serve at any time of day!

DOUGHNUTS IN HONEY SYRUP

SERVES 6

scant 2 cups white bread flour

1 tsp salt

finely grated rind of 1 orange

1^1/$_2$ tsp active dry yeast

1^1/$_4$ cups tepid water, plus 1 tbsp

^{1}/$_2$ cup honey

1 tsp lemon juice

sunflower-seed oil, for deep-frying

ground cinnamon, for sprinkling

These little fritters are delicious served as a dessert or as an afternoon snack–especially for children.

Put the flour, salt, and orange rind in the bowl of an electric mixer fitted with a dough hook and sprinkle in the yeast. Gradually add the water and whisk for 10 minutes to form a thick batter. Alternatively, make the batter in a large bowl using a hand-held electric whisk or balloon whisk. Cover the bowl with a clean dish towel and leave in a warm place for 2 hours, or until risen with lots of bubbles.

Meanwhile, to make the honey syrup, put the honey, lemon juice, and 1 tablespoon water in a pan and simmer until combined. Set aside.

When the batter has risen, heat the oil in a deep-fat fryer or deep pan to 350-375°F/180-190°C, or until a cube of bread browns in 30 seconds. Using 2 teaspoons (one to scoop and one to push), dip the spoons in cold water to prevent the batter from sticking and drop small amounts of the batter into the hot oil. Cook about 5 at a time for 2-3 minutes, turning with a slotted spoon, until puffed up and golden brown. Remove with the slotted spoon and drain on paper towels.

Serve about 5 hot doughnuts per person, spoon over the warm honey syrup, and sprinkle with cinnamon.

DOUGHNUT TWISTS

Heat the water, butter, brown sugar, orange rind, if using, and salt in a heavy-bottom pan over medium heat until the butter has melted.

Add the flour, all at once, the cinnamon and vanilla extract, then remove from the heat and beat rapidly until the mixture pulls away from the side of the pan.

Let cool slightly, then beat in the eggs, one at a time, beating well after each addition, until the mixture is thick and smooth. Spoon into a pastry bag fitted with a wide star tip.

Heat the oil for deep-frying in a deep-fat fryer or deep pan to 350–375°F/180–190°C, or until a cube of bread browns in 30 seconds. Pipe 5-inch/13-cm lengths about 3 inches/7.5 cm apart into the oil. Cook for 4 minutes, or until golden brown. Remove with a slotted spoon and drain on paper towels.

Dust the doughnuts with superfine sugar and cinnamon and serve either hot from the pan or cooled to room temperature.

SERVES 4

1 cup water

7 tbsp butter or shortening, diced

2 tbsp light brown sugar

finely grated rind of 1 small orange (optional)

pinch of salt

1¼ cups all-purpose flour, sifted

1 tsp ground cinnamon, plus extra for dusting

1 tsp vanilla extract

2 eggs

vegetable oil, for deep-frying

superfine sugar, for dusting

This Mexican-style doughnut has a very appealing shape. The dough is piped into lengths, which twist into a variety of interesting shapes when deep-fried. They go equally well with a cup of hot chocolate or a coffee.

GERMAN FRUIT BREAD

Oil a cookie sheet.

Put the currants, raisins, candied peel, and cherries in a bowl. Stir in the rum and set aside. Put the butter, milk, and superfine sugar in a pan and heat gently until the sugar has dissolved and the butter has just melted. Let cool until hand-hot. Sift the flour, salt, nutmeg, and cinnamon together into a bowl. Crush the cardamom seeds with a pestle in a mortar and add to the flour mixture. Stir in the yeast. Make a well in the center and add the milk mixture, lemon rind, and egg. Beat to form a soft dough.

Turn out the dough onto a lightly floured counter. With floured hands, knead the dough for 5-10 minutes—it will be quite sticky, so add more flour if necessary. Knead the soaked fruit and almonds into the dough until just combined. Return the dough to the clean, lightly oiled bowl. Cover with plastic wrap and let rise in a warm place for up to 3 hours, or until doubled in size. Turn out the dough again and knead lightly for 1-2 minutes. Roll out into a 10-inch/25-cm square.

Roll the marzipan into a sausage shape slightly shorter than the length of the dough and position down the center. Fold one side over to cover the marzipan. Repeat with the other side, overlapping in the center. Seal the ends. Transfer the roll, seam-side down, to the prepared cookie sheet. Cover with oiled plastic wrap and let prove in a warm place until doubled in size. Preheat the oven to 375°F/190°C.

Bake the bread in the preheated oven for 40 minutes, or until golden and it sounds hollow when tapped on the base. Brush the hot bread generously with melted butter and dredge heavily with confectioners' sugar. Transfer to a cooling rack and let cool completely.

This is a spiced German fruit bread with a marzipan filling, which is traditionally served at Christmas.

SERVES 10

oil, for oiling

scant $5/8$ cup currants

generous $1/3$ cup raisins

scant $1/4$ cup candied peel

2 oz/55 g candied cherries, rinsed, dried, and quartered

2 tbsp dark rum

4 tbsp butter, plus extra, melted, for brushing

$3/4$ cup milk

3 tbsp golden superfine sugar

$2^1/3$ cups white bread flour, plus extra for dusting

$1/2$ tsp salt

$1/2$ tsp ground nutmeg

$1/2$ tsp ground cinnamon

seeds from 3 green cardamom pods

2 tsp active dry yeast

finely grated rind of 1 lemon

1 egg, beaten

$3/8$ cup slivered almonds

6 oz/175 g ready-made marzipan

sifted confectioners' sugar, for dusting

FRUITY BREAD

SERVES 15

scant 5 cups strong white bread flour,
  plus extra for dusting

1 tsp ground allspice

1 tsp salt

2 tsp active dry yeast

1/4 cup golden superfine sugar

1 1/4 cups tepid milk, plus extra for
  brushing

2/3 cup tepid water

vegetable oil, for brushing

4 tbsp butter, softened, plus extra
  for greasing

11 1/2 oz/325 g dried mixed fruit

Sift the flour, allspice, and salt into a warmed bowl, then stir in the yeast and 1 tablespoon of the superfine sugar. Make a well in the center and pour in the milk and water. Mix well, gradually incorporating the dry ingredients to make a sticky dough. Place onto a lightly floured counter and knead the dough until no longer sticky. Brush a clean, warmed bowl with oil, place the dough in the bowl, cover with plastic wrap and let rise in a warm place for 1 hour, or until doubled in size.

Turn out the dough out onto a floured counter and knead lightly for 1 minute. Add the butter and mixed fruit to the dough and work them in well. Return the dough to the bowl, replace the plastic wrap and let rise for 30 minutes. Grease a 9-inch/23-cm round cake pan. Shape the dough into a neat round and fit in the pan. Cover and let prove in a warm place until it has risen to the top of the pan. Preheat the oven to 400°F/200°C.

Brush the top of the loaf lightly with milk and bake in the preheated oven for 15 minutes. Cover the loaf with foil, reduce the oven temperature to 350°F/180°C and bake for 45 minutes, or until the bread is golden and sounds hollow when tapped on the base. Transfer to a cooling rack and let cool.

This spiced bread was traditionally baked with a wedding ring thrown into the mixture in the belief that whoever found it would be married within the year.

TROPICAL FRUIT BREAD

Grease a cookie sheet.

Sift the flour, salt, and ginger together into a large warmed bowl. Stir in the bran, yeast, and sugar. Rub in the butter with your fingertips until the mixture resembles bread crumbs. Add the water and mix to form a dough.

Turn out the dough on to a lightly floured counter and knead for 5-10 minutes, or until smooth and elastic. Put the dough in a greased bowl, cover with plastic wrap, and let rise in a warm place for 30 minutes, or until doubled in size.

Turn out the dough again and knead in the pineapple, mango, and coconut. Shape into a circle and transfer to the prepared cookie sheet. Score the top with the back of a knife. Cover with plastic wrap and let prove in a warm place for 30 minutes. Preheat the oven to 425°F/220°C.

Brush the loaf with the beaten egg and sprinkle with coconut. Bake in the preheated oven for 30 minutes, or until golden brown.

Transfer the bread to a cooling rack and let cool before serving.

MAKES 1 LOAF

2 tbsp butter, diced, plus extra
   for greasing

2^1/$_3$ cups white bread flour, plus extra
   for dusting

^{1}/$_2$ tsp salt

^{1}/$_2$ tsp ground ginger

^{1}/$_2$ cup bran

1^1/$_2$ tsp active dry yeast

2 tbsp light brown sugar

generous 1 cup tepid water

2 oz/55 g candied pineapple, finely
   chopped

2 tbsp finely chopped dried mango

generous ^{1}/$_2$ cup grated coconut,
   toasted, plus extra for sprinkling

1 egg, lightly beaten

The flavors in this fruit bread will bring a touch of sunshine to your table, whatever the time of year. To test the bread after the second proving, gently prod the dough with your finger–it should spring back if it has proved enough.

MANGO TWIST BREAD

This is a sweet bread that has puréed mango mixed into the dough, resulting in a moist loaf with an exotic flavor.

MAKES 1 LOAF

3 tbsp butter, diced, plus extra for greasing

1 lb/450 g white bread flour, plus extra for dusting

1 tsp salt

1 tsp ground ginger

1 ^{1}/2 tsp active dry yeast

^{1}/4 cup light brown sugar

1 small mango, peeled, seeded, and blended to a purée

1 cup tepid water

2 tbsp honey

^{2}/3 cup golden raisins

1 egg, lightly beaten

confectioners' sugar, for dusting

Grease a cookie sheet. Sift the flour, salt, and ginger together into a large warmed bowl. Stir in the yeast and brown sugar. Rub in the butter with your fingertips until the mixture resembles bread crumbs. Stir in the mango purée, water, and honey and mix to form a dough.

Turn out the dough onto a lightly floured counter and knead for 5-10 minutes, or until smooth and elastic. Put the dough in a greased bowl, cover with plastic wrap, and let rise in a warm place for 1 hour, or until doubled in size.

Turn out the dough again and knead in the golden raisins. Shape the dough into 2 sausage shapes, each 10 inches/25 cm long. Carefully twist the 2 pieces together and pinch the ends to seal. Transfer to the prepared cookie sheet, cover, and let prove in a warm place for 40 minutes. Preheat the oven to 425°F/220°C.

Brush the loaf with the beaten egg. Bake in the preheated oven for 30 minutes, or until golden brown. Transfer to a cooling rack and let cool. Dust with confectioners' sugar before serving.

FRUIT AND NUT LOAF

Lightly grease a cookie sheet. Sift the flour and salt together into a warmed bowl. Rub in the margarine with your fingertips until the mixture resembles bread crumbs. Stir in the sugar, dried fruit, nuts, and yeast.

Warm the orange juice in a pan over low heat, but do not let it boil. Stir into the flour mixture with the yogurt. Mix to form a dough.

Turn out the dough onto a lightly floured counter and knead for 5-10 minutes, or until smooth and elastic. Shape into a circle and transfer to the prepared cookie sheet. Cover with a clean dish towel and let rise in a warm place for 1 hour, or until doubled in size. Preheat the oven to 425°F/220°C.

Bake the loaf in the preheated oven for 35-40 minutes, or until it sounds hollow when tapped on the base. Transfer to a cooling rack and brush the top of with the apricot jelly. Let cool before serving.

MAKES 1 LOAF

1 tbsp margarine, plus extra
   for greasing

scant 2 cups white bread flour, plus
   extra for dusting

1/2 tsp salt

2 tbsp light brown sugar

2/3 cup golden raisins

1/3 cup no-soak dried
   apricots, chopped

1/2 cup chopped hazelnuts

2 tsp active dry yeast

6 tbsp orange juice

6 tbsp plain yogurt

2 tbsp strained apricot jelly

This fruit bread may be served warm or cold, perhaps spread with a little butter, or topped with apricot jelly.

CHOCOLATE BREAD

Lightly grease a 2-lb/900-g loaf pan.

Sift the flour, salt, and cocoa together into a large bowl. Stir in the yeast and sugar. Make a well in the center. Add the oil and water to the well and mix to form a dough.

Turn out the dough onto a lightly floured counter and knead for 5–10 minutes, or until smooth and elastic. Put the dough in an oiled bowl, cover with plastic wrap, and let rise in a warm place for 1 hour, or until doubled in size.

Turn out the dough again and knead lightly for 1 minute. Shape into a loaf. Transfer the dough to the prepared pan, cover and let prove in a warm place for 30 minutes. Preheat the oven to 400°F/200°C.

Bake the loaf in the preheated oven for 25–30 minutes, or until it sounds hollow when tapped on the base. Transfer the loaf to a cooling rack and let cool completely. Cut into thick slices and serve with butter.

MAKES 1 LOAF

butter, for greasing and to serve

1 lb/450 g white bread flour, plus extra for dusting

1 tsp salt

generous 1/4 cup unsweetened cocoa

1 1/2 tsp active dry yeast

2 tbsp light brown sugar

1 tbsp oil, plus extra for oiling

1 1/4 cups tepid water

For the chocoholics among us, this bread is not only great fun to make, it also has a fantastic chocolate flavor. This bread can be sliced and spread with butter, or it can be lightly toasted.

breads

One of the most therapeutic of all baking methods must surely be the kneading of bread dough. The following pages give a flavor of the many types and shapes of bread enjoyed around the world. The recipes include Italian and Indian breads and breads with extra ingredients such as yogurt or potato. So whether it is rolls, sticks, loaves, or flatbreads that take your fancy, rise to the occasion and enjoy the mesmerizing smell of freshly cooked bread.

WHITE BREAD

Grease a 2-lb/900-g loaf pan or 2 cookie sheets.

Sift the flour and salt together into a large warmed bowl. Stir in the yeast. Make a well in the center. Add the oil and water to the well and mix to form a soft dough.

Turn out the dough onto a lightly floured counter and knead for 5–10 minutes, or until smooth and elastic. Put the dough in an oiled bowl, cover with plastic wrap and let rise in a warm place for 1 hour, or until doubled in size.

Turn out the dough again and knead lightly. For a loaf, shape into a rectangle the length of the pan and 3 times the width. With the long sides facing you, fold the top one-third down to cover the middle third, then fold the bottom one-third up and over the top and press together. Transfer to the prepared pan, join-side down. Alternatively, to make buns cut the dough into 8 equal pieces, shape each piece into a circle, and space well apart on the prepared cookie sheets. Dust with a little extra flour for a softer crust. Cover and let prove in a warm place for 30 minutes, or until the loaf is well risen above the pan or the buns have doubled in size. Preheat the oven to 450ºF/230ºC.

If baking a loaf, bake in the center of the preheated oven for 25–30 minutes, or until it sounds hollow when tapped on the base. If the top is browning too much, reduce the temperature a little. For the buns, bake for 15–20 minutes, swapping the cookie sheets around halfway through the baking time.

Transfer to a cooling rack and let cool. Eat as fresh as possible.

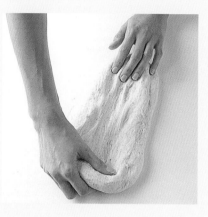

MAKES 1 LARGE LOAF OR 8 BUNS

butter, for greasing

1 lb/450 g white bread flour, plus extra
   for dusting

1 tsp salt

1¹/₂ tsp active dry yeast

1 tbsp vegetable oil, plus extra
   for oiling

1³/₄ cups tepid water

Bread is the staple food of many countries. In addition to the wide popularity of white bread, a variety of flours is used for making good-quality alternative breads, including organic and whole wheat flours.

PLAITED POPPY SEED BREAD

MAKES 1 LOAF

2 tbsp sunflower-seed oil, plus extra
   for oiling

1$\frac{1}{2}$ cups white bread flour, plus extra
   for dusting

2 tbsp skim milk powder

1 tsp salt

1$\frac{1}{4}$ tbsp sugar

$\frac{3}{4}$ cup hand-hot water

1 tsp active dry yeast

5 tbsp poppy seeds

TOPPING

1 egg yolk

1 tbsp milk

1 tbsp superfine sugar

2 tbsp poppy seeds

Oil a cookie sheet. Sift the flour into a large bowl, and add the milk powder, salt, and sugar. Pour in the water and oil. Make an indentation in the flour with your finger and add the yeast to it.

Lightly flour a counter. Knock the dough back gently and knead lightly for 1-2 minutes. Add the poppy seeds.

Divide the dough into 3 equal pieces and shape each piece into a rope about 10-12 inches/25-30 cm long. Place the ropes side by side and pinch them together at one end. Plait the dough, and pinch the other end together, tucking it underneath. Place the plait on the cookie sheet, cover with lightly oiled plastic wrap, and set aside in a warm place for about 30 minutes to rise. Preheat the oven to 400°F/200°C.

To make the topping, lightly beat the egg yolk with the milk and superfine sugar to combine. Remove the plastic wrap from the plait, brush the top with the egg glaze, and sprinkle over poppy seeds. Bake in the preheated oven for 30-35 minutes, until the loaf is golden and sounds hollow when tapped on the base. Transfer to a cooling rack and let cool.

If you are not used to plaiting, try practicing on the kitchen table with three tightly rolled-up dish towels.

MAKES 1 LOAF

butter, for greasing

generous 2¹/₃ cups white bread flour,
 plus extra for dusting

scant 1 cup rye flour

1¹/₂ tsp salt

1 tsp active dry yeast

1 tbsp light brown sugar

1¹/₂ tbsp skim milk powder

1 tsp caraway seeds

¹/₂ tsp poppy seeds

¹/₂ tsp sesame seeds

1¹/₄ cups tepid water

1¹/₂ tbsp sunflower-seed oil, plus extra
 for oiling

2 tsp lemon juice

TOPPING

1 egg white

1 tbsp water

1 tbsp sunflower or
 pumpkin seeds (pepitas)

MIXED SEED BREAD

Grease a 2-lb/900-g loaf pan. Sift the flours and salt together into a large warmed bowl. Stir in the yeast, sugar, milk powder, and seeds. Make a well in the center. Mix the water, oil, and lemon juice together and add to the well. Mix to form a dough.

Turn out the dough onto a lightly floured counter and knead for 5-10 minutes, or until smooth and elastic. Put the dough into an oiled bowl, cover with plastic wrap, and let rise in a warm place for 1 hour, or until doubled in size.

Turn out the dough again and knead lightly. Shape into a loaf and transfer to the prepared pan. Cover and let prove in a warm place for 30 minutes. Preheat the oven to 425°F/220°C.

To make the topping, lightly beat the egg white with the water. Brush over the top of the loaf, then gently press the seeds all over the top. Bake in the preheated oven for 25-30 minutes, or until it sounds hollow when tapped on the base. Transfer to a cooling rack and let cool.

FRENCH STICK

Lightly oil a cookie sheet.

Sift the flour and salt together into a large warmed bowl. Stir in the yeast. Make a well in the center. Add the water to the well and mix to form a soft dough.

Turn out the dough onto a lightly floured counter and knead for 5-10 minutes, or until smooth and elastic. Put the dough in an oiled bowl, cover with plastic wrap, and let rise in a warm place for 1 hour, or until doubled in size.

Turn out the dough again and knead lightly. Cut the dough in half. Shape each half into a ball. Roll out each ball into a rectangle measuring 3 x 8 inches/7.5 x 20 cm. With the long sides of one rectangle facing you, fold one-third down to cover the middle third, then fold the bottom third up and over the top and press together. Set aside to rest while you repeat with the second rectangle. Repeat twice more with each rectangle, leaving to rest between each folding.

Lightly flour and pleat 2 clean dish towels. Gently roll and stretch each piece of dough, in turn, into a stick about 12 inches/30 cm long. Put each baguette between the pleats of a dish towel to support it and cover with lightly oiled plastic wrap. Let prove in a warm place for 30-40 minutes. Preheat the oven to 450°F/230°C.

Gently roll the loaves from the dish towels onto the prepared cookie sheet, spaced well apart. Make several diagonal slashes on the tops with a sharp knife. Spray the preheated oven with water and bake the loaves for 15-20 minutes until crusty and golden. Transfer to a cooling rack and let cool. Eat as fresh as possible.

MAKES 2

oil, for oiling

1 lb/450 g white bread flour,
   plus extra for dusting

1½ tsp salt

1½ tsp active dry yeast

generous 1¼ cups tepid water

The first sign of quality in a baguette is a hard crust of a rich, dark caramel color. The texture of a good baguette should be moist.

WHITE BUNS

MAKES 10

oil, for oiling

1 lb/450 g white bread flour, plus extra
  for dusting

1¹/₂ tsp salt

1 tsp active dry yeast

2 tsp superfine sugar

generous ¹/₂ cup tepid water

generous ¹/₂ cup tepid milk

milk, for glazing

Lightly oil 2 cookie sheets.

Sift the flour and salt together into a large warmed bowl. Stir in the yeast and sugar. Make a well in the center. Add the water and milk to the well and mix to form a soft dough.

Turn out the dough onto a lightly floured counter and knead for 5–10 minutes, or until smooth and elastic. Put the dough in an oiled bowl, cover with plastic wrap, and let rise in a warm place for 1 hour, or until doubled in size.

Turn out the dough again and knead lightly.

Cut the dough into 10 equal pieces, shape each piece into a ball, then roll out into a 4-inch/10-cm long oval. Space the ovals well apart on the prepared cookie sheets and cover with lightly oiled plastic wrap. Let prove in a warm place for 30 minutes. Preheat the oven to 400°F/200°C.

Gently press the center of each bun with 2 fingers to release any large air bubbles, then brush the tops with milk and dust with a little extra flour for a softer crust.

Bake in the preheated oven for 15–20 minutes, or until lightly browned. Transfer the buns to cooling racks and let cool slightly. Serve warm.

You could shape your dough into a log and use a stiff spatula to divide it into equal portions. To be exact, weigh each piece of dough so the buns are the same size.

ENGLISH MUFFINS

Lightly flour a cookie sheet. Mix the yeast with half the water in a bowl until it has dissolved. Add the remaining water and the yogurt and mix well. Sift the flour and salt together into a large warmed bowl. Make a well in the center. Add the yeast mixture to the well and mix to form a soft dough.

Turn out the dough onto a lightly floured counter and knead for 5-10 minutes until smooth and elastic. Return to the bowl, cover with plastic wrap, and let rise in a warm place for 30-40 minutes, or until doubled in size.

Turn out the dough again and knead lightly. Roll out to a thickness of 3/4 inch/2 cm. Using a 3-inch/7.5-cm cutter, cut into 10-12 circles and sprinkle the semolina over each muffin. Transfer to the prepared cookie sheet, cover, and let prove in a warm place for 30-40 minutes.

Heat a griddle or a large skillet over medium-high heat. Lightly brush with oil. Add half the muffins and cook for 7-8 minutes on each side, taking care not to burn them. Repeat with the remaining muffins.

Serve freshly cooked with lots of butter. Muffins can be kept for up to 2 days in an airtight container. To reheat, split them across the center and quickly toast before serving with butter, and jelly, if you like.

MAKES 10-12

1 lb/450 g white bread flour, plus extra for dusting

2 x 1/6 oz/7 g active dry yeast

generous 1 cup tepid water

1/2 cup plain yogurt

1/2 tsp salt

1/4 cup fine semolina

vegetable oil, for brushing

TO SERVE

butter

jelly (optional)

If you do not have a round cutter, use a large mug to cut the muffins out of the dough.

MAKES 1 LOAF

1$^{1}/_{2}$ tbsp sunflower-seed oil, plus extra
   for oiling

scant 1$^{1}/_{2}$ cups whole wheat bread
   flour, plus extra for dusting

1 tsp salt

1 tsp active dry yeast

2 tbsp light brown sugar

1 tbsp skim milk powder

$^{3}/_{4}$ cup tepid water

You can tell if the loaf is ready,
because it should sound hollow when
you tap the base with your knuckles.

HARVEST LOAF

Oil a 2-lb/900-g loaf pan. Sift the flour and salt together into a warmed bowl. Stir in the yeast, sugar, and milk powder. Make a well in the center. Add the oil and water to the well and mix to form a soft dough.

Turn out the dough onto a lightly floured counter and knead for 5–10 minutes, or until smooth and elastic. Put in an oiled bowl, cover with plastic wrap, and let rise in a warm place for 1 hour, or until doubled in size.

Turn out the dough again and knead lightly. Shape into a loaf and transfer to the prepared pan. Cover and let prove in a warm place for 30 minutes. Preheat the oven to 425°F/220°C.

Bake in the preheated oven for 25–30 minutes, or until it sounds hollow when tapped on the base. Transfer to a cooling rack and let cool.

WHOLE WHEAT YOGURT BREAD

MAKES 1 LOAF

1 tbsp sunflower-seed oil, plus extra
for oiling

generous 1¼ cups white bread flour,
plus extra for dusting

1 cup whole wheat bread flour

1 tsp salt

½ cup wheat bran

¾ tsp active dry yeast

⅔ cup tepid water

½ cup plain yogurt, at
room temperature

1 tbsp molasses or corn syrup

The flour used should be at room
temperature. If your flour feels cold,
try warming it up in a low oven for
a few minutes.

Oil a cookie sheet. Sift the flours and salt together into a warmed bowl. Stir in the bran and yeast. Make a well in the center. Mix the water, yogurt, oil, and molasses together and add to the well. Mix to form a soft dough.

Turn out the dough onto a lightly floured counter and knead for 5–10 minutes, or until smooth and elastic. Put in an oiled bowl, cover with plastic wrap, and let rise in a warm place for 1 hour, or until doubled in size.

Turn out the dough again and knead lightly. Shape into a circle and transfer to the prepared cookie sheet. Cover and let prove in a warm place for 30 minutes. Preheat the oven to 425°F/220°C.

Bake in the preheated oven for 25–30 minutes, or until it sounds hollow when tapped on the base. Transfer to a cooling rack and let cool.

OATMEAL AND POTATO BREAD

Mealy potatoes have a soft, dry texture once cooked. A popular variety is the Russet.

MAKES 1 LOAF

oil, for oiling

8 oz/225 g mealy potatoes
   (peeled weight)

1 lb 2 oz/500 g white bread flour, plus
   extra for dusting

1¹/₂ tsp salt

3 tbsp butter, diced

1¹/₂ tsp active dry yeast

1¹/₂ tbsp dark brown sugar

3 tbsp rolled oats

2 tbsp skim milk powder

scant 1 cup tepid water

TOPPING

1 tbsp water

1 tbsp rolled oats

Oil a 2-lb/900-g loaf pan. Put the potatoes in a large pan, add water to cover, and bring to a boil. Cook for 20–25 minutes until tender. Drain, then mash until smooth. Let cool.

Sift the flour and salt into a warmed bowl. Rub in the butter with your fingertips. Stir in the yeast, sugar, oats, and milk powder. Mix in the mashed potato, then add the water and mix to a soft dough.

Turn out the dough onto a lightly floured counter and knead for 5–10 minutes, or until smooth and elastic. Put the dough in an oiled bowl, cover with plastic wrap, and let rise in a warm place for 1 hour, or until doubled in size.

Turn out the dough again and knead lightly. Shape into a loaf and transfer to the prepared pan. Cover and let prove in a warm place for 30 minutes. Preheat the oven to 425°F/220°C.

Brush the surface of the loaf with the water and carefully sprinkle over the oats. Bake in the preheated oven for 25–30 minutes, or until it sounds hollow when tapped on the base. Transfer to a cooling rack and let cool slightly. Serve warm.

SODA BREAD

Preheat the oven to 425ºF/220ºC. Oil a cookie sheet.

Sift the flour, salt, and baking soda together into a large bowl. Make a well in the center. Add most of the buttermilk to the well and, using your hands, mix to form a dough. The dough should be very soft but not too wet. Add the remaining buttermilk if necessary.

Turn out the dough onto a lightly floured counter and knead lightly. Shape into an 8-inch/20-cm circle.

Transfer the loaf to the prepared cookie sheet, cut a cross in the top, and bake in the preheated oven for 25–30 minutes, or until it sounds hollow when tapped on the base. Transfer to a cooling rack and let cool slightly. Eat while still warm. Soda bread is always best eaten the same day as it is baked.

MAKES 1 LOAF

oil, for oiling

1 lb/450 g all-purpose flour, plus extra
  for dusting

1 tsp salt

1 tsp baking soda

1³/4 cups buttermilk

Soda bread is a bread made without yeast. The raising agent is baking soda mixed with buttermilk. It is simple to make, needs very little kneading and no time at all for rising. The loaves are cut on the top into a cross shape to help the bread rise and, according to Irish folklore, to let the devils (or the fairies) out. Soda bread can be made with brown or white flour or a mixture of the two and is a wonderful partner for cheese and an ideal accompaniment to soup.

RYE AND SEED BREAD

Oil a 2-lb/900-g loaf pan. Sift all the flours and salt together into a large warmed bowl. Stir in the yeast, bread crumbs, bran, cocoa, and caraway seeds. Make a well in the center. Mix the water, oil, and molasses together, add to the well and mix to form a soft dough.

Turn out the dough onto a lightly floured counter and knead for 5–10 minutes, or until smooth and elastic. Put the dough in an oiled bowl, cover with plastic wrap, and let rise in a warm place for 1 hour, or until doubled in size.

Turn out the dough again and knead lightly. Shape into a loaf and transfer to the prepared pan. Cover and let prove in a warm place for 30 minutes. Preheat the oven to 425°F/220°C.

Bake the loaf in the preheated oven for 25–30 minutes, or until it sounds hollow when tapped on the base. Transfer to a cooling rack and let cool.

MAKES 1 LOAF

2 tbsp sunflower-seed oil, plus extra
    for oiling

scant $^2/_3$ cups white bread flour, plus
    extra for dusting

1 cup rye flour

$^1/_2$ cup whole wheat flour

$1^1/_2$ tsp salt

$^1/_2$ tsp active dry yeast

generous $^2/_3$ cup dried bread crumbs

3 tbsp oat bran

$1^1/_2$ tbsp unsweetened cocoa

2 tsp caraway seeds

generous $1^1/_2$ cups tepid water

$2^1/_2$ tbsp molasses

Made from a cereal grass, rye flour has less gluten than all-purpose or whole wheat flour. It is heavier and darker in color than most flours and produces dense bread. The most common form is medium rye flour, available in supermarkets.

BREADSTICKS

Lightly oil 2 cookie sheets.

Sift the flour and salt together into a warmed bowl. Stir in the yeast. Make a well in the center. Add the water and oil to the well and mix to form a soft dough.

Turn out the dough onto a lightly floured counter and knead for 5-10 minutes, or until smooth and elastic. Put the dough in an oiled bowl, cover with plastic wrap, and let rise in a warm place for 1 hour, or until doubled in size.

Turn out the dough again and knead lightly. Roll out into a rectangle 9 x 8 inches/23 x 20 cm. Cut the dough into 3 strips, each 8 inches/20 cm long, then cut each strip across into 10 equal pieces.

Gently roll and stretch each piece of dough into a stick about 12 inches/30 cm long. Spread the sesame seeds out on a large, shallow plate or tray. Roll each breadstick in the sesame seeds to coat, then space well apart on the prepared cookie sheets. Brush with oil, cover with plastic wrap, and let prove in a warm place for 15 minutes. Preheat the oven to 400°F/200°C.

Bake the breadsticks in the preheated oven for 10 minutes. Turn over and bake for an additional 5-10 minutes until golden. Transfer to a cooling rack and let cool.

MAKES 30

3 tbsp olive oil, plus extra for oiling and brushing

generous 2^{1}/$_{8}$ cups white bread flour, plus extra for dusting

1^{1}/$_{2}$ tsp salt

1^{1}/$_{2}$ tsp active dry yeast

scant 1 cup tepid water

sesame seeds, for coating

Breadsticks are the ideal accompaniment to soup or salad. For added flavor, try adding some Parmesan cheese and fresh or dried rosemary to your breadstick mix before making the dough.

FOCACCIA WITH MOZZARELLA AND ROSEMARY

This is an extremely versatile flatbread. As well as baking it plain, you could bake it with toppings such as cheese, onion, roasted bell peppers, and sun-dried tomatoes.

MAKES 1 LOAF

1 tbsp olive oil, plus extra for oiling

generous 2¹/₂ cups white bread flour, plus extra for dusting

¹/₂ tsp salt

1 tsp active dry yeast

1 tsp sugar

scant 1 cup tepid water

5 oz/140 g mozzarella cheese, grated

TOPPING

2 tbsp olive oil

fresh rosemary sprigs

coarse sea salt

Lightly oil a 10-inch/25-cm round shallow cake pan.

Sift the flour and salt together into a warmed bowl. Stir in the yeast and sugar. Make a well in the center. Add the water and oil to the well and mix to form a soft dough.

Turn out the dough onto a lightly floured counter and knead for 5-10 minutes, or until smooth and elastic. Put the dough in an oiled bowl, cover with plastic wrap, and let rise in a warm place for 1 hour, or until doubled in size.

Turn out the dough again and knead lightly. Flatten the dough, then sprinkle over the mozzarella cheese and gently knead in. Shape into a ball, flatten slightly, then roll out into a 10-inch/25-cm circle. Transfer to the prepared pan, cover with lightly oiled plastic wrap, and let prove in a warm place for 20 minutes.

Make deep indentations all over the surface of the dough with your fingers. Cover with lightly oiled plastic wrap and let prove in a warm place for an additional 15 minutes. Preheat the oven to 400°F/200°C.

To make the topping, drizzle the oil all over the surface of the dough, then sprinkle with rosemary sprigs and sea salt. Bake in the preheated oven for 20-25 minutes until golden. Transfer to a cooling rack and let cool slightly. Serve warm.

CIABATTA WITH TOMATO AND BASIL

MAKES 2 LOAVES

SPONGE MIXTURE

generous 1 cup white bread flour

$^{1}/_{2}$ tsp active dry yeast

scant 1 cup tepid water

DOUGH

generous 2 cups white bread
   flour, plus extra for dusting

$1^{1}/_{2}$ tsp salt

$^{1}/_{4}$ tsp active dry yeast

$^{1}/_{2}$ tsp sugar

scant 1 cup tepid water

2 tbsp olive oil, plus extra for oiling

2 tbsp milk

$1^{1}/_{2}$ oz/40 g drained sun-dried
   tomatoes in oil, coarsely chopped,
   plus extra for topping (optional)

2 tbsp shredded fresh basil

To make the sponge, sift the flour into a warmed bowl. Stir in the yeast. Make a well in the center. Add the water and mix into the flour mixture. Cover with plastic wrap and leave in a warm place overnight or for 12 hours.

To make the dough, sift the flour and salt together into a separate bowl. Stir in the yeast and sugar. Make a well in the center. Add the water, oil, and milk to the sponge mixture and mix together, then add to the well and mix to form a dough.

Turn out the dough onto a lightly floured counter and knead for 5-10 minutes, or until smooth and elastic. Knead in the sun-dried tomatoes and basil. Put the dough in a large bowl, cover with lightly oiled plastic wrap, and let rise in a warm place for 1 hour.

Lightly flour 2 cookie sheets. Halve the dough, using a spoon, and gently tip each half onto a prepared cookie sheet. Shape each piece into a rectangular loaf about 1 inch/2.5 cm thick. Dust with flour and leave, uncovered, to prove in a warm place for 30 minutes. Preheat the oven to 425°F/220°C.

Sprinkle extra sun-dried tomatoes over the tops of the loaves, if you like. Bake in the preheated oven for 25-30 minutes until the loaves are golden. Transfer to a cooling rack and let cool.

Ciabatta dough should be almost batter-like and very sticky. Ciabatta, requires a "sponge," which is a type of yeast that gives the bread its uniquely tangy flavour.

OLIVE BREAD

This olive-enriched bread is ideal to serve with appetizers, or to accompany soups. Choose either black or green olives, according to your preference.

Lightly oil a cookie sheet. Sift the flour and salt together into a large bowl. Stir in the yeast, 2 teaspoons of the sesame seeds, and the oregano. Make a well in the center. Add the water and oil to the well and mix to form a firm dough.

Turn out the dough onto a lightly floured counter and knead for 10 minutes, or until smooth and elastic. Put the dough in a bowl, cover with a clean, damp dish towel, and let rise in a warm place for 1 hour, or until doubled in size.

Turn out again and knead lightly, then knead in the olives. Cut the dough in half and shape each half into a smooth circle. Transfer to the prepared cookie sheet, cover with a clean dish towel, and let prove in a warm place for 30 minutes. Preheat the oven to 425°F/220°C.

Using a sharp knife, make slashes across the top of each loaf. Lightly brush with oil and sprinkle with the remaining sesame seeds. Bake in the preheated oven for 10 minutes. Reduce the temperature to 375°F/190°C. Bake for an additional 25 minutes, or until golden and the loaves sound hollow when tapped on the base. Let cool on a cooling rack.

MAKES 2 MEDIUM LOAVES

- 3 tbsp olive oil, plus extra for oiling and brushing
- 2 lb/900 g white bread flour, plus extra for dusting
- 1 tsp salt
- 1¹/₂ tsp active dry yeast
- 3 tsp sesame seeds
- ¹/₂ tsp dried oregano
- 2¹/₂ cups warm water
- 8 oz/225 g olives, pitted and coarsely chopped

PITA BREAD

Lightly oil a cookie sheet.

Sift the flour and salt together into a warmed bowl. Stir in the yeast and sugar. Make a well in the center. Add the water and oil to the well and mix to form a dough.

Turn out the dough onto a lightly floured counter and knead for 5-10 minutes, or until smooth and elastic. Put the dough in an oiled bowl, cover with plastic wrap, and let rise in a warm place for 1 hour, or until doubled in size.

Turn out the dough again and knead lightly. Cut the dough into 6 equal pieces and shape each piece into a ball. Transfer to the prepared cookie sheet. Cover with oiled plastic wrap and let prove in a warm place for 10 minutes. Put 2-3 cookie sheets in the oven and preheat the oven to 450°F/230°C.

Flatten each piece of dough slightly, then roll out each piece into a circle. Sprinkle lightly with flour and cover with plastic wrap. Leave for 10 minutes to rest.

Transfer the dough circles to the hot cookie sheets, spaced well apart, and bake in the preheated oven for 5 minutes, or until risen and golden. Transfer to a cooling rack and let cool.

MAKES 6

1 tbsp olive oil, plus extra for oiling

generous 2$^{1}/_{8}$ cups white bread flour, plus extra for dusting

1$^{1}/_{2}$ tsp salt

1 tsp active dry yeast

1 tsp sugar

scant 1 cup tepid water

NAAN BREAD

These leavened breads have been baked in India since the days of Moghul rule, traditionally by slapping the rolled and shaped dough against the hot inside of a charcoal-heated tandoor oven. Without the benefit of a tandoor oven, you need to preheat your oven with a cookie sheet inside to its highest setting in plenty of time.

MAKES 10

2 lb/900 g white bread flour

1 tbsp baking powder

1 tsp sugar

1 tsp salt

1¼ cups water, heated to 122°F/50°C

1 egg, beaten

4 tbsp ghee, melted, plus extra for
    rolling out and brushing

Sift the flour, baking powder, sugar, and salt together into a large bowl. Make a well in the center. Beat the water and egg together in a bowl. Gradually add to the well, using your fingers to draw in the flour from the side, until a stiff, heavy dough forms. Shape the dough into a ball and return it to the bowl.

Soak a clean dish towel in hot water, then wring it out and use it to cover the bowl, tucking the ends of the towel under the bowl. Let rest for 30 minutes.

Turn out the dough onto a counter brushed with melted ghee and flatten the dough. Gradually sprinkle with the melted ghee and knead in, little by little. Shape the dough into 10 equal balls.

Resoak the towel in hot water and wring it out again, then place it over the dough balls. Let rise in a warm place for 1 hour. Put 1–2 cookie sheets in the oven and preheat the oven to 450°F/230°C or its highest setting.

Use a lightly greased rolling pin to roll the dough balls into teardrop shapes, about ⅛ inch/3 mm thick. Lightly rub the hot cookie sheets with ghee. Transfer the naans to the hot cookie sheets and bake in the preheated oven for 5–6 minutes until golden brown and lightly puffed. Brush the hot naans with melted ghee and serve immediately.

CHAPATIS

MAKES 6

**1¹/₂ cups whole wheat flour, sifted,
plus extra for dusting**

¹/₂ tsp salt

²/₃-scant 1 cup water

melted ghee, for brushing

This is the everyday bread for millions
of Indians, eaten by virtually everyone
from the richest to the very poor. The
soft, malleable texture makes these
flatbreads ideal for mopping up
"gravies," as Indian sauces are known,
and for scooping up bite-sized
portions of food, doing away with
knives and forks. Unleavened chapatis
are traditionally made with *atta*, a type
of Indian whole wheat flour that is
sold in Asian food stores and some
large supermarkets, but ordinary
whole wheat flour is fine if you sift out
the gritty pieces of bran first.

Sift the flour and salt together into a large bowl. Make a well in the
center. Gradually stir in enough water to make a stiff dough.

Turn out the dough onto a lightly floured counter and knead for
10 minutes, or until smooth and elastic. Shape into a ball and put in a
bowl. Cover with a damp dish towel and let rest for 20 minutes.

Cut the dough into 6 equal pieces. Lightly flour your hands and roll
each piece into a ball. Heat a large, ungreased tava, skillet, or griddle
over high heat until very hot and a splash of water "dances" when it hits
the surface.

Working with one dough ball at a time, flatten, then roll out into a
7-inch/18-cm circle. Add to the hot pan and cook until brown flecks
appear on the bottom. Flip over and cook on the other side.

Flip the dough over again and use a bunched-up dish towel to press
down all around the edge. This pushes the steam in the chapati around,
causing the chapati to puff up. Continue cooking until the bottom
is golden brown, then flip over and repeat on the other side.

Brush the chapati with melted ghee and serve. Repeat with the
remaining dough balls. Chapatis are best served immediately, but they
can be kept warm, wrapped in foil, for 20 minutes.

pies, savory flans, AND pizza

Pies and flans know few boundaries: sweet or savory, meat or vegetarian, and baked in short-crust, suet, choux, or puff pastry. As well as the more traditional recipes such as Apple Pie and Fish in Pastry, here you will find more contemporary options such as Sweet Potato Pie and Key Lime Pie, and variations such as Peach Cobbler. The more adventurous pastry fan can try their hand at a Mushroom Gougère or a batch of Bleu Cheese and Walnut Tartlets and to top it off, there are even recipes for that ever popular dish, the pizza.

APPLE PIE

Grease a 9-inch/23-cm round fluted tart pan.

Sift the flour and salt together into a bowl. Rub in the butter with your fingertips until the mixture resembles fine bread crumbs. Rub in the cheese. Lightly beat the egg yolks and water together, then add to the mixture and mix to form a soft dough.

Turn out the dough onto a lightly floured counter. Knead lightly until smooth. Wrap in foil or plastic wrap and chill in the refrigerator for 30 minutes. Preheat the oven to 400°F/200°C.

Roll out two-thirds of the dough and use to line the prepared pan. Layer in the sliced apples with all but 1 teaspoon of the sugar and the spices.

Roll out the remaining dough, dampen the edges of the dough lining the pan, and lay the rolled dough on top. Press down well to seal the edges and cut away any excess dough. Crimp the edges with the tines of a fork.

Beat the egg white in a small bowl and use to glaze the pie, sprinkling the remaining sugar over to give a crisp finish.

Bake in the preheated oven for 40–45 minutes until the pastry is crisp and golden.

Cut the pie into portions and slip a slice of cheese under the crust of each piece before serving.

SERVES 6-8

butter, for greasing

generous 2³/₈ cups all-purpose flour,
   plus extra for dusting

pinch of salt

7 tbsp butter, diced and chilled

3¹/₂ oz/100 g mild cheese, grated

2 egg yolks

3 tbsp cold water

2 lb/900 g cooking apples, peeled,
   cored, and thinly sliced

generous ¹/₂ cup superfine sugar

¹/₂ tsp ground cinnamon

¹/₂ tsp ground cloves

1 egg white

6 oz/175 g mild cheese, sliced,
   to serve

This recipe uses mild cheese in the dough and also serves a little extra with the hot pie so that it melts while being eaten. You will not need any cream.

KEY LIME PIE

Preheat the oven to 325°F/160°C. Lightly grease a 9-inch/23-cm round pie plate, about 1¹/₂ inches/4 cm deep.

To make the crumb crust, put the crackers, sugar, and cinnamon into a food processor and process until fine crumbs form—do not overprocess to a powder. Add the butter and process again until the crumbs are moistened.

Tip the crumb mixture into the pie plate and press over the base and up the side. Transfer the pie plate to a cookie sheet and bake in the preheated oven for 5 minutes.

Meanwhile, beat the condensed milk, lime juice, lime rind, reserving some for decorating, and egg yolks together in a bowl until well blended.

Remove the crumb crust from the oven, pour the filling into the crumb crust, and spread out to the edge. Bake for an additional 15 minutes, or until the filling is set around the edge but still wobbly in the center. Transfer to a cooling rack and let cool completely, then cover and chill in the refrigerator for at least 2 hours. Serve with dollops of whipped cream and decorate with the reserved lime rind.

SERVES 6-8

CRUMB CRUST

6 tbsp butter, melted, plus extra for greasing

6 oz/175 g graham crackers or ginger cookies

2 tbsp superfine sugar

¹/₂ tsp ground cinnamon

FILLING

1³/₄ cups condensed milk

¹/₂ cup freshly squeezed lime juice

finely grated rind of 3 limes

4 large egg yolks

freshly whipped cream, to serve

Tart and creamy, this classic American pie is ideal for summer entertaining. Commercial key lime pies have green food coloring added, but this recipe is undoctored and so has a pale cream color.

SWEET POTATO PIE

To make the pie dough, sift the flour, salt, and sugar into a bowl. Rub in the butter and white vegetable fat with your fingertips until the mixture resembles fine bread crumbs. Sprinkle over 2 tablespoons of the water and mix to form a soft dough. If the dough seems dry, add the extra 1/2 tablespoon water. Wrap in foil or plastic wrap and chill in the refrigerator for at least 1 hour.

Meanwhile, to make the filling, bring a large pan of water to a boil over high heat. Add the sweet potatoes and cook for 15 minutes. Drain, then cool under cold running water. When cool, peel, then mash. Put the sweet potatoes in a bowl and beat in the eggs and sugar until very smooth. Beat in the remaining ingredients, then cover and set aside until required.

When ready to bake, preheat the oven to 425°F/220°C. Roll out the dough on a lightly floured counter into a thin 11-inch/28-cm circle and use to line a 9-inch/23-cm round pie plate, about 1 1/2 inches/4 cm deep. Trim off the excess dough and press the floured tines of a fork around the edge.

Prick the base of the pastry shell all over with the fork and put a piece of crumpled foil in the center. Bake in the preheated oven for 12 minutes, or until lightly golden.

Remove the the foil, pour the filling into the pastry shell, and bake for an additional 10 minutes. Reduce the temperature to 325°F/160°C and bake for an additional 35 minutes, or until a knife inserted into the center comes out clean. Transfer to a cooling rack and let cool. Serve warm or at room temperature with whipped cream.

Serve slices of this pie and see if guests can guess the main ingredient. Few people will expect the humble sweet potato to be turned into such a rich, indulgent dessert.

SERVES 8-10

PIE DOUGH

scant 1 1/4 cups all-purpose flour, plus extra for dusting

1/2 tsp salt

1/4 tsp superfine sugar

3 tbsp butter, diced and chilled

3 tbsp white vegetable fat, diced and chilled

2-2 1/2 tbsp iced water

FILLING

1 lb 2 oz/500 g orange-fleshed sweet potatoes, scrubbed

3 extra-large eggs, beaten

generous 1/2 cup light brown sugar

1 1/2 cups evaporated milk

3 tbsp butter, melted

2 tsp vanilla extract

1 tsp ground cinnamon

1 tsp ground nutmeg or freshly grated nutmeg

1/2 tsp salt

freshly whipped cream, to serve

FOREST FRUIT PIE

SERVES 4

FILLING

2 cups fresh blueberries

2 cups fresh raspberries

2 cups fresh blackberries

1 cup superfine sugar

2 tbsp confectioners' sugar,
   to decorate

whipped cream, to serve

PASTRY

1^1/$_2$ cups all-purpose flour, plus extra
   for dusting

^{1}/$_4$ cup ground hazelnuts

scant ^{1}/$_2$ cup unsalted butter, diced
   and chilled, plus extra for greasing

finely grated rind of 1 lemon

1 egg yolk, beaten

4 tbsp milk

Pick over the berries and put in a pan with 3 tablespoons of the superfine sugar and cook over a medium heat, stirring frequently, for 5 minutes. Remove from the heat.

To make the pie dough, sieve the flour into a bowl, then stir in the hazelnuts. Rub in the butter with your fingertips until the mixture resembles bread crumbs, then sieve in the remaining superfine sugar. Add the lemon rind, egg yolk, and 3 tablespoons of the milk and mix to form a dough. Turn out onto a lightly floured work surface and knead briefly. Wrap with plastic wrap and let chill in the refrigerator for 30 minutes.

Preheat the oven to 375ºF/190ºC. Grease an 8-inch/20-cm pie dish with butter. Roll out two-thirds of the pie dough to a thickness of ^{1}/$_4$-inch/5 mm and use it to line the base and side of the dish. Spoon the berries into the case. Brush the rim with water, then roll out the remaining pie dough and use it to cover the pie. Trim and crimp round the edge, then make 2 small slits in the top and decorate with 2 leaf shapes cut out from the pie dough trimmings. Brush all over with the remaining milk. Bake in the preheated oven for 40 minutes.

Dust the pie with the confectioners' sugar and serve with whipped cream.

RHUBARB CRUMBLE

Preheat the oven to 375ºF/190ºC.

Cut the rhubarb into 1-inch/2.5-cm lengths and put in a 7¼-cup ovenproof dish with the superfine sugar and orange rind and juice.

To make the crumble, sift the flour into a bowl. Rub in the butter with your fingertips until the mixture resembles fine bread crumbs. Stir in the brown sugar and ginger. Spread evenly over the fruit and press down lightly with a fork.

Transfer the dish to a cookie sheet and bake in the center of the preheated oven for 25-30 minutes until the crumble is golden brown.

Serve warm with cream, yogurt, or custard.

SERVES 6

2 lb/900 g rhubarb

generous ½ cup superfine sugar

grated rind and juice of 1 orange

cream, yogurt, or custard, to serve

CRUMBLE

scant 1⅝ cups all-purpose or
    whole wheat flour

8 tbsp butter, diced and chilled

generous ½ cup light brown sugar

1 tsp ground ginger

Crumble is one of the simplest puddings, easy to make, and delicious to eat. The first, forced shoots of rhubarb are the sweetest and the most tender. Ginger is often added to improve the flavor, but a little orange really adds to the taste. The crumble topping can be made with white or brown flour, and some nuts may be added, if you like.

PEACH COBBLER

Preheat the oven to 425°F/220°C. Put the peaches in a 9-inch/23-cm square ovenproof dish that is also suitable for serving. Add the sugar, lemon juice, cornstarch, and almond extract and toss together. Bake the peaches in the preheated oven for 20 minutes.

Meanwhile, to make the topping, sift the flour, all but 2 tablespoons of the sugar, the baking powder, and salt together into a bowl. Rub in the butter with your fingertips until the mixture resembles fine bread crumbs. Mix the egg with 5 tablespoons of the milk in a pitcher, add to the mixture, and mix with a fork to form a soft, sticky dough. If the dough seems dry, stir in the extra tablespoon of milk.

Reduce the oven temperature to 400°F/200°C. Drop spoonfuls of the topping over the surface, without smoothing. Sprinkle with the

remaining sugar and bake for an additional 15 minutes, or until the topping is golden brown and firm —the topping will spread as it cooks.

Serve the cobbler hot or at room temperature with ice cream on the side.

SERVES 6

6 peaches, peeled, pitted, and sliced

4 tbsp superfine sugar

1/2 tbsp lemon juice

1 1/2 tsp cornstarch

1/2 tsp almond extract or vanilla
  extract

vanilla or pecan nut ice cream,
  to serve

COBBLER TOPPING

scant 1 1/4 cups all-purpose flour

generous 1/2 cup superfine sugar

1 1/2 tsp baking powder

1/2 tsp salt

6 tbsp butter, diced and chilled

1 egg

5-6 tbsp milk

Summertime in Georgia means peaches and more peaches. This old-fashioned baked dessert with its "cobblestone" topping is a traditional way to take advantage of the seasonal glut.

PEAR PIE

SERVES 6

PIE DOUGH

scant 2 cups all-purpose flour

pinch of salt

scant 2/3 cup superfine sugar

4 oz/115 g butter, cut into pieces

1 egg and 1 egg yolk

few drops vanilla extract

2-3 tsp water

sifted confectioners' sugar,
   for sprinkling

FILLING

4 tbsp apricot preserve

2 oz/55 g amaretti or ratafia cookies,
   crumbled

1 lb 14 oz-2 lb 4 oz/850 g-1 kg pears,
   peeled and cored

1 tsp ground cinnamon

1/2 cup raisins

1/3 cup packed brown or raw sugar

To make the dough, sift the flour and salt onto a counter, make a well in the center, and add the sugar, butter, egg, egg yolk, vanilla extract, and most of the water.

Using the fingers, gradually work the flour into the other ingredients to form a smooth dough, adding more water if necessary. Wrap the dough and let chill in the refrigerator for at least 1 hour.

Preheat the oven to 400°F/200°C. Roll out three-quarters of the dough and use to line a shallow 10-inch/25-cm cake pan or deep tart pan. To make the filling, spread the preserve over the base and sprinkle with the crushed cookies.

Slice the pears very thinly. Arrange over the cookies in the pastry shell. Sprinkle with cinnamon, then with raisins, and finally with brown sugar.

Roll out a thin sausage shape using one-third of the remaining pie dough, and place around the edge of the pie. Roll the remainder into thin sausages and arrange in a lattice over the pie, 4 or 5 strips in each direction, attaching them to the strip around the edge.

Cook in the preheated oven for 50 minutes until golden brown and cooked through. Let cool, then serve the pie warm or chilled, sprinkled with sifted confectioners' sugar.

Pears are very popular in desserts. In this recipe they are flavored with almonds, cinnamon, raisins, and apricot preserve. Choose ripe pears that are still firm. Don't peel and slice them in advance or the flesh will discolor and spoil the appearance of the dessert.

FISH IN PASTRY

Preheat the oven to 400°F/200°C. Grease a 5-cup pie dish.

Put the fish in a skillet and cover with the milk. Add the bay leaf, peppercorns, and onion slices. Bring to a boil, then reduce the heat and simmer gently for 10-12 minutes.

Remove from the heat and pour off the milk into a measuring cup. Add a little extra milk if necessary to make the liquid up to 1¼ cups. Flake the fish into large pieces, removing any bones.

Melt the butter in a pan over low heat and add the flour. Cook, stirring constantly, for 2-3 minutes. Remove from the heat and gradually stir in the reserved milk, beating well after each addition. Return the pan to the heat and cook, stirring constantly, until thickened. Cook for an additional 2-3 minutes until smooth and glossy. Season to taste with salt and pepper and stir in the parsley and cream.

Put the fish in the base of the prepared pie dish, then add the egg and season to taste with salt and pepper. Pour the sauce over the fish and mix gently.

Roll out the pastry on a lightly floured counter until just larger than the pie dish. Cut off a strip ½ inch/1 cm wide around the edge. Moisten the rim of the dish with water and press the pastry strip onto it. Moisten the pastry collar and put on the pastry lid. Crimp the edges firmly and glaze with the beaten egg. Garnish with the leftover pastry shaped into leaves, if you like.

Transfer the pie to a cookie sheet and bake near the top of the preheated oven for 20-25 minutes. Cover with foil if getting too brown.

Creamy fish and flaky pastry is a marriage made in heaven. This recipe suggests using white fish fillets, but you can use other fish if you prefer–a mixture of haddock and smoked haddock is good.

SERVES 4-6

3 tbsp butter, plus extra for greasing

1 lb 7 oz/650 g white fish fillets, such as cod or haddock, skinned

1½ cups milk

1 bay leaf

4 peppercorns

1 small onion, finely sliced

scant ⅓ cup all-purpose flour, plus extra for dusting

salt and pepper

1 tbsp chopped fresh parsley or tarragon

⅔ cup light cream

2 hard-cooked eggs, coarsely chopped

14 oz/400 g ready-made flaky pastry, thawed if frozen

1 egg, beaten, to glaze

MUSHROOM GOUGÈRE

Preheat the oven to 400°F/200°C. Grease a round ovenproof dish.

To make the pastry, sift the flour and salt together onto a sheet of waxed paper. Put the water and butter in a pan over low heat and heat until the butter has melted. Bring to a rolling boil. Remove from the heat and add the flour, all at once, beating well until the mixture leaves the side of the pan and forms a ball. Let cool slightly. Gradually beat in the eggs until the dough is smooth and glossy. Beat in the cheese. Spoon the pastry around the side of the prepared dish.

To make the filling, heat the oil in a large, heavy-bottom skillet over medium heat. Add the onion and cook, stirring frequently, for 5 minutes, or until softened. Add the mushrooms and garlic and cook, stirring, for 2 minutes. Stir in the flour and cook, stirring constantly, for 1 minute. Gradually stir in the stock. Bring to a boil, stirring constantly, and cook for 3 minutes, or until thickened. Set aside 2 tablespoons of the walnuts. Stir the remainder into the mushroom mixture with the chopped parsley. Season to taste with salt and pepper.

Spoon the filling into the center of the dish and sprinkle over the remaining walnuts. Bake in the preheated oven for 40 minutes, or until the pastry is risen and golden. Serve at once.

SERVES 4

CHOUX PASTRY

4 tbsp butter, plus extra for greasing

scant $^{1}/_{2}$ cup white bread flour

pinch of salt

$^{2}/_{3}$ cup water

2 eggs

2 oz/55 g Emmental cheese, grated

FILLING

2 tbsp olive oil

1 onion, chopped

8 oz/225 g cremini mushrooms, sliced

2 garlic cloves, finely chopped

1 tbsp all-purpose flour

$^{2}/_{3}$ cup vegetable stock

$^{3}/_{4}$ cup walnuts, chopped

2 tbsp chopped fresh parsley

salt and pepper

LEEK AND SPINACH QUICHE

SERVES 6-8

2 tbsp unsalted butter, plus extra for
   greasing

9 oz/250 g ready-made puff pastry,
   thawed if frozen

all-purpose flour, for dusting

2 leeks, finely sliced

8 oz/225 g fresh spinach leaves,
   chopped

2 eggs

1¼ cups heavy cream

pinch of dried thyme

salt and pepper

Grease an 8-inch/20-cm round fluted tart dish. Roll out the pastry on a lightly floured counter and let rest for 5 minutes. Use to line the tart dish so that a little pastry overhangs evenly all round the edge. Cover and let chill in the refrigerator while you make the filling.

Preheat the oven to 350°F/180°C.

Melt the butter in a large skillet over medium heat. Add the leeks and cook, stirring frequently, for 5 minutes, or until softened. Add the spinach to the mixture and cook for 3 minutes, stirring frequently, until wilted. Let cool.

Beat the eggs in a bowl. Stir in the cream, thyme, and salt and pepper to taste. Spread the cooked vegetables over the base of the pastry shell. Pour in the egg mixture.

Transfer the tart dish to a cookie sheet and bake in the preheated oven for 30 minutes, or until set. Let rest for 10 minutes before serving. Serve directly from the tart dish.

TOMATO AND GRUYÈRE TART

SERVES 6

scant 1⅝ cups all-purpose flour, plus
extra for dusting

8 tbsp butter or margarine, diced and
chilled

3–4 tbsp iced water

2 tbsp oil

2 onions, sliced

4 oz/115 g Gruyère cheese, grated

10 oven-dried tomato halves

1¼ cups heavy cream

2 large eggs

handful of fresh chives, snipped

salt and pepper

few fresh thyme sprigs, to garnish

Grease an 8-inch/20-cm round fluted tart dish. Sift the flour into a large bowl. Rub in the butter with your fingertips until the mixture resembles fine bread crumbs. Add enough of the water to mix to a firm dough. Roll out on a lightly floured counter and use to line the tart dish so that a little pastry overlaps evenly all round the edge. Prick the base of the pastry shell all over with a fork and let chill in the refrigerator for 1 hour.

Preheat the oven to 400°F/200°C.

Heat the oil in a skillet over medium heat. Add the onions and cook, stirring frequently, for 10-15 minutes, or until browned. Meanwhile, put a piece of crumpled foil in the center of the pastry shell and bake in the preheated oven for 12 minutes. Remove the foil and bake for an additional 5 minutes, or until just golden. Transfer the onions to the pastry shell and sprinkle over the cheese. Arrange the tomatoes on top.

Beat the cream, eggs, and chives together in a bowl. Season well with salt and pepper and pour into the pastry shell. Reduce the oven temperature to 350°F/180°C and bake for 30-35 minutes until set and browned. Garnish with thyme sprigs and serve.

BLEU CHEESE AND WALNUT TARTLETS

Lightly grease a 3-inch/7.5-cm 12-hole muffin pan. Sift the flour and the celery salt together into a food processor, add the butter, and process until the mixture resembles fine bread crumbs. Alternatively, rub the fat into the flour mixture in a bowl with your fingertips. Tip into a large bowl and add the walnuts and enough iced water to form a firm dough.

Turn out onto a lightly floured counter and cut the dough in half. Roll out one half. Using a 3-1/2 inch/9-cm pastry cutter, cut out 6 circles. Roll out each round to 4^{1}/2 inches/12 cm in diameter and use to line half the muffin holes. Repeat with the remaining dough. Line each hole with parchment paper and fill with baking beans. Let chill in the refrigerator for 30 minutes. Preheat the oven to 400°F/200°C.

Bake the tartlet cases in the preheated oven for 10 minutes. Remove from the oven, then remove the paper and beans.

To make the filling, melt the butter in a skillet over medium-low heat. Add the celery and leek and cook, stirring occasionally, for 15 minutes until very soft. Add 2 tablespoons cream, crumble in the cheese, and mix well. Season to taste with salt and pepper. Put the remaining cream in a pan and bring to simmering point. Pour onto the egg yolks in a heatproof bowl, stirring constantly. Mix in the cheese mixture and spoon into the tartlet shells.

Bake for 10 minutes, then turn the pan around and bake for an additional 5 minutes. Let the tartlets cool in the pan for 5 minutes. Serve garnished with parsley.

This is a good pie dough for sweet or savory dishes.
Hazelnuts and pecans also work well but do not overchop the nuts; they should only be chopped finely enough to combine well with the dough.

MAKES 12

WALNUT PIE DOUGH

7 tbsp butter, diced and chilled,
    plus extra for greasing

scant 1^{5}/8 cups all-purpose flour, plus
    extra for dusting

pinch of celery salt

^{1}/4 cup walnut halves, chopped

FILLING

2 tbsp butter

2 celery stalks, finely chopped

1 small leek, finely chopped

scant 1 cup heavy cream,
    plus 2 tbsp

7 oz/200 bleu cheese

3 egg yolks

salt and pepper

chopped fresh flat-leaf parsley and
    parsley sprigs, to garnish

SPRING VEGETABLE TART

SERVES 4

PIE DOUGH

9 tbsp butter, diced and chilled, plus
   extra for greasing

scant 2 cups all-purpose flour, plus
   extra for dusting

pinch of salt

generous $3/8$ cup freshly grated
   Parmesan cheese

1 egg

FILLING

$10^1/2$ oz/300 g mixed baby spring
   vegetables, such as carrots,
   asparagus, peas, fava beans, salad
   onions, corn, and leeks

$1^1/4$ cups heavy cream

$4^1/2$ oz/125 g sharp Cheddar cheese,
   grated

2 eggs, plus 3 egg yolks

handful of fresh tarragon and flat-leaf
   parsley, chopped

salt and pepper

Grease a 10-inch/25-cm round loose-bottom tart pan. Sift the flour and the salt together into a food processor, add the butter, and process until the mixture resembles fine bread crumbs. Alternatively, rub the fat into the flour mixture in a bowl with your fingertips. Tip into a large bowl and stir in the Parmesan cheese. Beat the egg and a little iced water together in a small bowl. Add most of the egg mixture and mix to form a soft dough, adding more if necessary.

Turn out onto a lightly floured counter. Roll out into a circle $3^1/4$ inches/8 cm larger than the pan and use to line the pan. Roll the rolling pin over the pan to neaten and trim the edge. Line the tart shell with parchment paper and fill with baking beans. Let chill in the refrigerator for 30 minutes. Preheat the oven to 400°F/200°C.

Bake the tart shell in the preheated oven for 15 minutes. Remove the paper and beans and bake for an additional 5 minutes. Remove from the oven and let cool. Reduce the oven temperature to 350°F/180°C.

Prepare the vegetables as necessary, then cut into bite-sized pieces. Bring a large pan of lightly salted water to a boil. Add the vegetables and blanch for 2 minutes. Drain and let cool. Put the cream in a separate pan and bring to simmering point. Put the Cheddar cheese, eggs, and egg yolks in a heatproof bowl and pour over the hot cream. Add the herbs and salt and pepper to taste and stir to combine. Arrange the vegetables in the tart shell, pour over the cheese custard, and bake for 30-40 minutes until just set. Let cool in the pan for 10 minutes before serving.

Use only the most tender young vegetables for this tart. If they are really small, you can leave them whole. A few slices of soft goat cheese can be added just before baking.

FOUR SEASONS PIZZA

MAKES 2 X 6-INCH/15-CM PIZZAS

oil, for oiling

9 oz/250 g ready-to-make pizza
    dough mix

TOMATO SAUCE

2 tbsp olive oil

1 small onion, finely chopped

1 garlic clove, finely chopped

1 red bell pepper, seeded and chopped

8 oz/225 g plum tomatoes, peeled
    and chopped

1 tbsp tomato paste

1 tsp light brown sugar

1 tbsp shredded fresh basil leaves

1 bay leaf

salt and pepper

TOPPING

2$^{1}/_{2}$ oz/70 g canned or bottled anchovy
    fillets, drained and halved lengthwise

2 oz/55 g artichoke hearts, thinly sliced

1 oz/25 g mozzarella cheese, sliced

1 tomato, thinly sliced

3$^{1}/_{2}$ oz/100 g mushrooms, thinly sliced

2 tsp capers, rinsed

2 tsp pitted, sliced black olives

2 tbsp olive oil

salt and pepper

Lightly oil a cookie sheet. To make the tomato sauce, heat the oil in a heavy-bottom pan over low heat. Add the onion, garlic, and red bell pepper and cook, stirring occasionally, for 5 minutes, or until softened. Add the tomatoes, tomato paste, sugar, basil, and bay leaf and season to taste with salt and pepper. Cover and simmer, stirring occasionally, for 30 minutes. Remove from the heat and let cool completely.

Make up the dough according to the package directions. Once risen, shape into 2 equal circles about $^{1}/_{4}$ inch/5 mm thick. Transfer to the prepared cookie sheet, cover with plastic wrap and let rise in a warm place for 20-30 minutes. Preheat the oven to 400°F/200°C.

Spread the tomato sauce over the pizza bases, almost to the edge. Cover one quarter of each with anchovy fillets. Cover a second quarter with sliced artichoke hearts. Cover the third quarters with alternate slices of mozzarella cheese and tomato. Cover the final quarters with sliced mushrooms. Sprinkle with the capers and olives, season to taste with salt and pepper, and drizzle with oil. Bake in the oven for 15-20 minutes, or until the cheese has browned and the bases have risen.

TOMATO AND PEPPERONI PIZZA

**MAKES 4 X 6-INCH/
15-CM PIZZAS**

1 tbsp olive oil, plus extra for oiling

1 lb 2 oz/500 g ready-to-make
   pizza dough mix

2 tbsp green pesto

2 onions, sliced

2 oz/55 g pepperoni slices

5^1/$_2$ oz/150 g mozzarella cheese, torn
   into pieces

8 oz/225 g cherry tomatoes, halved

12 olives

few fresh basil leaves

pepper

mixed salad, to serve

Lightly oil a large cookie sheet.

Make up the dough according to the package directions. Once risen, shape into 4 equal circles about ^{1}/$_4$ inch/5 mm thick. Transfer to the prepared cookie sheet, cover with plastic wrap, and let rise in a warm place for 20-30 minutes. Preheat the oven to 400°F/200°C.

Spread the pesto over the pizza bases, almost to the edge. Heat the oil in a large skillet over medium heat. Add the onions and cook, stirring frequently, for 3-4 minutes until softened. Sprinkle over the pizza bases. Arrange the pepperoni and cheese slices on top, then tuck in the cherry tomato halves. Sprinkle the olives and basil over the top and season well with pepper.

Bake the pizzas in the preheated oven for 15-20 minutes, or until the cheese has browned and the bases have risen. Serve immediately with a mixed salad.

INDEX